MW01244166

Life-Changing Stories
Reflections of a Seasoned Therapist

Dr. Terry Parsons

Copyright 2019

Life-Changing Stories
Reflections of a Seasoned Therapist

Copyright 2019 © Terry Parsons
All rights Reserved

No part of this book may be reproduced or transmitted in any form or by any means, electronic or mechanical, including photocopying and recording or by any information storage or retrieval system.
Cover and interior design by Sidewalk Labs.

Requests for permission should be addressed to
ttparsons@aol.com

ISBN-13: 9781675545386

About the Author:

Dr. Terry Parsons earned a Ph.D. in Clinical Psychology, a Masters in Theology, and a Doctorate in Pastoral Care and Counseling. He draws from his thirty years of experience as a therapist in Dallas, Texas, and from his earlier years as a hospital chaplain and church minister. Dr. Parsons holds teaching and consulting positions at Southern Methodist University's Perkins School of Theology. He leads seminars and retreats for premarital and married couples, and he is the author of *The Intimacy Jungle: How You Can Survive and Thrive in a Lasting Marriage.*

CONTENTS

ACKNOWLEDGEMENTS

I am grateful to the many people who have helped me in so many ways to write this book. While they are deceased, my treasured mentors have laid the foundation for my work. Reverend David E. Erb (1929-2018), hospital chaplain and John H. Gladfelter, Ph.D. (1926-2012), clinical psychologist. Their influence inspires me every day.

Many people have read these stories and provided valuable suggestions, editing, and support. I am so appreciative for their help. Dr. Justin Tull, minister and coach; Janette Tull, music teacher and Stephen Minister; Karen Long, writing teacher; Elizabeth Hamilton, writer; Susan Swanson, M.D, ophthalmologist; John Everhart, retired business owner; Melody Fortenberry, Ph.D., psychologist; Denise Humphrey, Ph.D, psychologist; Laura Parsons Chester, daughter and child and family therapist; Michelle Kimzey, Ph.D., nursing school professor; John Patredis, counselor and life coach; Dr. Isabel Docampo, seminary professor; Meredith Scruggs, seminary student; Reverend Sandy Heard, minister; Reverend Mary

Lessman, priest; Dr. Don Underwood, minister; Debbie Beneke, counseling intern; Morris Bryant, M.D., medical school professor; Nancy Umphres, psychotherapist; Dr. Clayton Oliphint, my pastor; Aaron Stout, technical support and creative design; and Kathleen Parsons, beloved wife and my computer expert.

My thanks to the amazing people who are the subjects of these stories and the people I am privileged to have counseled through the years. They have taught me so much!

INTRODUCTION

You have had many experiences in your life, and some of them have been life-changing. The stories in this book are about some life-changing experiences I've shared with people in my thirty years as a therapist (and forty years as a minister). I invite you to travel with me to the front porch, hospital rooms, and my therapy office for some insights, inspiration, and practical help.

The first stories come from my early years as a student minister and hospital chaplain intern when I learned some important and sometimes painful lessons about being a caring and effective person. The remaining stories are about people I've traveled with as their therapist. It has been a privilege and a blessing to accompany them on their journeys. The identities and descriptions of these amazing people have been carefully guarded to preserve their privacy.

Following each story are questions for your reflection and application and some timely quotes on the topic. A *Study Guide* in the back of the book offers you the opportunity to delve deeper into to the stories with questions designed for your personal, professional, or group work.

Whether you are personally struggling, interested in helping others, or you work in a helping profession, I hope these stories about some remarkable people will offer you insights and useful information, touch your heart, and inspire you to do good for yourself and others.

Shalom,

Terry Parsons

Meet People Where They Are

The following story is about a learning experience that has profoundly influenced me, and I believe can speak to all of us. A brief paraphrase from Leo Tolstoy's short story "The Three Questions" succinctly describes these points. 1) Now is the most important time because it is the only time when we have any power. 2) The most necessary person is the one with whom we are. 3) The most important act is to do good because that is our purpose.

WON'T YOU BE MY NEIGHBOR?

He was a crusty old farmer sitting on his front porch with a bulging jaw full of chewing tobacco. I was barely twenty, still wet behind the ears, making my first pastoral visit as a student minister. I introduced myself to him and invited him to come to church. He gave me a cold stare and said, "Hell will freeze over before I go across the road to that church!"

Then he spat a huge wad of tobacco into the flower bed. I did not know what do or say. Finally, I managed, "Well if you ever change your mind, you are welcome to come."

I turned slowly and was walking down the porch steps onto the brick walk when he called out, "Boy, you're the first preacher who's had enough guts to come over here."

I simply nodded my head and crossed the road to the little church. It had not taken any guts to go see the man. I was just doing what I thought I should do. I was an earnest, but naïve student minister.

I never went back to visit him.

LIFE IN THE REAR VIEW MIRROR

One year later, as I stood beside my car after my last Sunday at the little one-room church with an average attendance of eight people, I waved to him. He slowly raised his hand to tip his hat to me. I drove away, but I never forgot that man.

If I had known then what I know now, I would have gone back to visit him. But at the time, I was too afraid. Also, I had not cared enough about him as a person—as a neighbor—to think how I could get to know him or minister to him.

USING OUR FEAR

"*Courage is fear plus action*," has become one of my favorite quotes. I wish I had had enough courage or faith or compassion to go back and visit this man.

Fear can be real or imagined. If that man had a loaded shotgun pointed at me, that would have been a *real* scary situation. In that case, my life could have been in danger. But my fear on the farmer's front porch was my own sense of inadequacy, and because of it, I walked away.

Paul Tillich's book *The Courage to Be* speaks about the state of "being grasped by God" rather than by fear. Fear can control our lives, but faith and courage can help us reach out into the unknown or step forward with a spirit of confidence.

Knowing what I now know, I would have gone back to visit him and *met him where he was*. I would have asked him some caring questions, so I could come to understand him. I would have asked him to tell me about his family and his farm. I would have talked with him about the weather and his crops. When a church member told me about the issue behind his resentful resolve, I would have said to him, "I'm new here, so I'd appreciate your telling me about the family dispute over the name of the community and the church."

These would have been invitations for him to share with me about his life, not an obligatory invitation for him to come to a church that represented hurt and bitterness rather than love and compassion.

He may never have come to church, but I hope he would have known I cared about him.

Walking in Another's Shoes

We do not always know what people carry inside or how they will respond when we reach out to them. If we don't meet people where they are, we miss the opportunity to get to really know them.

Having grown up on a farm myself, I knew people like him. If I'd simply visited with him like a farm neighbor rather than a potential church member, I think the conversation would have led to us sitting on the porch together and having a good visit. He was probably a good and interesting person who had been deeply offended by the change of the name of the community and the church.

I blew my chance to get to know him and possibly to be helpful. I have often wondered what happened to him and what I could have done?

During my year preaching once a month at that little church, I delivered sermons about God's love and the commandment to love others. Most Sunday mornings, he sat on his porch across the road from the church with folded arms and stared at us.

What if I had had the courage to visit him again? I do not know the answer to this question, but this experience made a strong impression on me and helped me to muster more courage and care to reach out and meet people where they are.

Maybe hell doesn't have to freeze over before a life-changing, "I will go across the road."

One of my friends, John Everhart, reminds me that *experience is the most valuable commodity.* Well, my first pastoral visit was quite a memorable learning experience.

Within this story are principles that are important for all of us as we learn, grow, and live our lives with struggles and opportunities.

- Have the courage and care to "cross the road" to reach out to people.
- Meet and accept people where they are and get to know them.
- Have the compassion to help people who are in need.

WORDS TO LIVE BY

"When you meet anyone, treat the event as a holy encounter." Wayne Dyer

Jesus met people where they were: the fishermen who became disciples at their nets; Matthew the tax collector at his table; the Samaritan woman with five husbands at the well; Martha and Mary at their home, etc.

FOR PERSONAL REFLECTION:

- How can this story be helpful to you?
- What do you think about meeting people where they are?

For more questions see the Study Guide in the back of the book.

We are so busy, focused on taking care of other people, or simply being neglectful, that we fail to take care of ourselves. People who carry a heavy load of responsibility and persons in helping professions seem to be especially prone to this condition. The following story was a life-lesson for me in my first week of training as a hospital chaplain.

SELF-CARE

After one week of orientation for Clinical Pastoral Education Internship at Presbyterian Hospital in Dallas, with three other seminary interns, I volunteered to take the first week as the "on call" chaplain. While visiting one of my units, my pager "beeped," and I called the hospital switchboard to tell me the nature of the call. "Chaplain, ER needs you there immediately."

I raced down three flights of stairs to the emergency room with no idea what awaited me. "We have a fourteen-year-old boy in here from a motorcycle accident," said the ER nurse. "It looks bad...probably dead. We'll see what we can do. Come in if you can handle it." There he was, a slender boy with massive head injuries lying lifelessly. Doctors and nurses were doing everything possible to save his life. A few minutes later, another nurse came to the trauma room door and said, "Chaplain, the boy's parents are here. You can meet with them in the family room."

VISITING EMOTIONS

There they were. Distraught parents pacing with clinched fists and tearful moans drawn from the depth of their souls. As I entered the room, the dad started pounding the wall with his fists, and the mom limply fell to the floor weeping. I gently knelt by her and put my hand on her shoulder. I told them I was a chaplain. They frantically asked if I knew anything. I said that the doctors and nurses were doing everything they could for their son. I asked their son's name and they said, "Johnny."

For the next hour, I went back and forth between the trauma room and the small family room to give reports to the parents. By this time, the ER waiting room was filled with Johnny's teen-aged friends. I learned that Johnny and some friends were riding their dirt bikes in a field when Johnny hit a tree headfirst without a helmet. His friends said he was a good boy who made excellent grades in school, had loads of friends, and loved the adventure and excitement of riding his dirt bike.

DEEPEST REGRETS

"If only he had worn his helmet!" his mom cried. During that hour with Johnny's family and friends, I comforted them as best I could. When I went back to the trauma room, the physically and emotionally exhausted trauma team shook their heads and the ER doctor said, "He's gone. God knows we did everything we could, but he was dead when he arrived. We tried and tried, but we just could not get him back. I'll go with you to tell the parents."

The ER doctor told the parents they did everything they could, but they could not bring their son back to life. He said some medical terms about the trauma, but the parents were already in a glazed state of shock. After the doctor left, I sat with the parents and their seventeen-year-old daughter. I said I was so sorry for them. I asked if they would like to see Johnny and they replied, "Oh, yes."

The parents had a brief, somber "visit" with their beloved dead son. Then, they mechanically completed the obligatory paperwork, consented for their son to be taken to the medical examiner for an autopsy, and chose a funeral home. We tightly held each other, and I prayed with them. I walked with them to the waiting room where Johnny's friends embraced them. Eventually, I accompanied them to their pickup truck in the ER parking area. I watched them drive away and I cried, "Oh, God!"

I slowly walked back into the hospital where I found the ER staff members outside the trauma room. One weary nurse said, "Welcome to our world." We talked for a few minutes. Now, I was physically and emotionally spent. I felt sad for Johnny's family and friends. I felt sad for the ER staff. I felt sad for Johnny who had died so young. I just felt sad, very sad.

A WORLD APART

The next thing I knew, I was wandering up the back stairs in a dazed state. I opened a door. I saw babies. There must have been twenty of them. I had entered the newborn nursery. I walked around the glass perimeter looking at the babies wrapped in pink and blue blankets with identifying names, birth times, weights, and measurements. I must have stayed there for fifteen or twenty minutes. The nurses smiled and nodded at me. This is the irony of a hospital. A short time apart people are experiencing the most horrible and the most joyful times of their lives.

A few weeks after Johnny's death, I received a letter in the chaplain's office. It was from Johnny's parents. I read it and felt grateful and sad. They had written how much they appreciated my help at the worst time in their lives. My chaplain supervisor, Dave Erb, read the note and said, "Make a file right now and put this note in it. There will be times when you will need to pull it out and read it."

SAVING AFFIRMATIONS

He was right. That note and my visits to the newborn nursery helped me cope with traumas, deaths, stresses, and other problems during my years as a hospital chaplain. I made it a daily practice to visit the newborn nursery. There I witnessed new life and the peaceful sleep of precious little babies.

I experienced and learned a lot during those first days, weeks, and months as a student chaplain. One of the most important lessons I learned was that it is crucial to take care of ourselves. Whether it is families such as Johnny's who experience such traumatic loss, the professionals who care for them, or any one of us, we must take care of ourselves. We all need to do this...not selfishly, just healthily. Jesus said to love others as ourselves. For people who give so much to others, it is important to love ourselves as we love others.

STAYING SANE

Over the years, many lessons have helped me stay sane through hard times and everyday life. One has been to have a mentor, counselor, or colleague with whom I can confide and share my stuff. Physical exercise, reading, art, sports, prayer, and having good friends also help. More recently, I've added writing, meditation, time at our family farm, and singing in the church choir. Through it all, my dear wife has been the love of my life, and our children and grandchildren have added more to my life than I could have imagined. Also, our series of dogs have proven to be just what the doctor ordered. I think they are God's gift of unconditional love. Currently, thirteen-year-old Teddy is our love.

A part of my personal philosophy is that I care deeply, but I try not to worry much. Worry helps no one. I do the best I can when I'm with a person. When we part, in a prayerful manner, I bid them to God's care. The Spanish words for good-bye, "Vaya con Dios" (Go with God) or "Adios" (to God) say it well.

TAKE CARE...

Self-care helps us to stay sane. Sane comes from the Latin word *sanus* that means "to be healthy physically and mentally." You can add to that definition other areas of your life, such as emotionally, professionally or vocationally, relationally, and spiritually. I encourage you to find ways to care for yourself that will work with your schedule. After all, self-care is a great investment of time that pays dividends in all areas of our lives. Self-care also allows one to have the energy and sanity to help others.

WORDS TO LIVE BY

"Take good care of yourself, you belong to Me."
God (My interpretation)

"Self-care is never a selfish act—it is simply good stewardship of the only gift I have, the gift I was put on earth to offer others." Parker Palmer

FOR PERSONAL REFLECTION:

- How can this story be helpful to you?
- What helps you to stay "sane"?

For more questions see the Study Guide in the back of the book.

Shut Up and Listen!

Is being a good listener one of your best traits? Most of us could be better. I believe listening is an art and skill that requires a lifetime of practice. It can be one of the greatest gifts we can give to others and to ourselves. The following story contains this simple, but profound exclamation that still rings in my ears: "Shut up and listen!"

LISTENING IS A SKILL

While I was a young and inexperienced seminary student beginning my training as a hospital chaplain intern, Dr. Simpson wanted to make sure I learned this very important skill.

As the head of the speech pathology department at the new neurology unit at Presbyterian Hospital in Dallas, Dr. Simpson especially wanted me to understand aphasia and its effect on those patients whose type of stroke made it difficult for them to speak. She explained in her very exacting manner:

"Aphasiac patients may have a thought in their brain, but it is very difficult for them to move their thought to the process necessary for speech. You may think you know what they want to say, and you will want to say it for them. Or they may begin a sentence and stop at some point because they cannot access the word necessary to complete their sentence. Again, you may want to help them, so you are tempted to complete the sentence for them. Do you understand what I am saying, Mr. Parsons?"

BE A PATIENT LISTENER

I said that I did. She stared at me for a long time with a serious expression. Finally, she said,

"Mr. Parsons, what I am telling you is that when working with aphasiac patients, you must not say the words for them. You must wait and be patient with them. You must let them find and form the words and express them. That is what they need to do. So, Mr. Parsons, what I am simply saying to you is that when you are working with aphasiac patients, you must shut up and listen!"

CRUCIAL FOR ALL RELATIONSHIPS

What she said was true. When the aphasiac patients were finally able to say the word they were searching for, or when they completed a sentence, a wonderful crooked smile would creep across their faces. Yes! Shut up and listen, and this would happen.

During my years working in the hospital, I remembered to shut up and listen. Now as a therapist, I can show my patients respect and concern the most by giving my undivided attention and listen to them.

For couples or families or friends, one of the most important skills for a healthy relationship is to know how to listen. When I lead marriage and premarital seminars, I focus on the importance of patiently listening to one another every day.

When I teach seminary students and ministers, I remind them that they will be better ministers and preachers if they really listen to people.

When I teach or mentor student counselors, I emphasize that one of the most important skills for our profession is to listen well to what people say and what they don't say.

When I'm with my wife, children, grandchildren, family members, and friends, I want to be a good listener.

A teacher reminded me that children often have no one who will listen to them. They are rarely asked their opinion. They are just told what to wear, what to do, and where to be.

LISTEN WITH ALL YOUR SENSES

It is also important not only to listen with our ears, but all our senses. This helps us "listen" to the whole person: their facial expressions and tears, their posture and gestures, their folded arms and smiles.

Never have I heard people complain that their mate, child, parent, sibling, friend, therapist, patient, minister, congregation, doctor, nurse, teacher, student, boss, employee, coach, athlete,

> *attorney, client, or animal listened to*
> *them too well. Never, have I heard that*
> *as a gripe. Never!*

LISTENING IS A GIFT

Whether in a personal or professional relationship, listening is one of the best gifts we can give to one another.

For most of us, being a good listener is not our greatest quality. It often takes extra effort to develop this art and skill. But listening with empathy or compassion conveys to people that we care about them. This often prompts them to share more freely and openly, and on a deeper level. And it is important to listen carefully to both their words and feelings. Listening to the whole person means that we are paying attention to their voice, words, tones, physical expressions, and to seemingly obvious items they do not verbalize. Being able to listen to them with caring acceptance is often a part of the healing experience which involves being heard, valued, and relieved.

AFFIRM AND ASK GOOD QUESTIONS

Affirming comments are a part of good listening. After hearing an especially painful story, I may say, "Thank you for sharing this with me. I know that you have carried this pain for a long time, and I admire your courage to share it."

Asking inviting questions is also crucial. This helps us gather information or gain a better understanding of the person. I may ask the person, "How long have you felt this way?" or simply say, "Tell me about it." Then, carefully listen to their response or story. People want to feel understood.

REWARDS OF LISTENING

Being a good listener can also help other people be more open to listen to us. Wouldn't it be great if a person thought or said about you, "You're really a good listener." When we really listen well to other people, they may even respond with a smile.

BE A GOOD LISTENER

❖ Listening is an art and a skill that requires practice.
❖ Listen with your ears and your eyes. (Give undivided attention.)
❖ Good listening means not letting our reaction or rebuttal get in the way.
❖ Good listening means not just being quiet but paying careful attention to the content and feelings that are being expressed. (Without distractions.)
❖ A good listener communicates "I care about you."
❖ A good listener communicates "I'm interested in you and what you say."
❖ A good listener is patient and considerate.
❖ A good listener waits until other people have formed their words and spoken.
❖ Being a good listener can be one of the best gifts you can give others and yourself.

WORDS TO LIVE BY

"I like to listen. I've learned a great deal from listening carefully. Most people never listen."   Ernest Hemingway

"Most of the successful people I've known are the ones who do more listening than talking." Bernard Baruch

"Most people do not listen with the intent to understand; they listen with intent to reply." Stephen R.

Covey

"Anyone with ears to hear should listen and understand." Jesus in Matthew 11:15

"You're short on ears and long on mouth." John Wayne

- How can this story be helpful to you?
- How well do you listen?

For more questions see the Study Guide in the back of the book.

If They Stay Married, It Will Be A Miracle

Are you aware of marriages that seem doomed to destruction? Some marriages cannot be saved. Others, when both people make profound changes, can work. This story is about one of those amazing couples whose mutual compassion saved their marriage.

"I killed my first husband," Martha said. It was then that I realized why the minister who had referred newlyweds Sam and Martha to me had noted, "If they don't kill each other, it will be amazing. If they stay married, it will be a miracle." Sam and Martha had each been married three times before. They hoped the fourth time would be the charm.

SEX, VIOLENCE AND DIVORCES

Martha had married for the first time when she was a seventeen-year-old high school dropout. She and her twenty-year-old husband abused alcohol and drugs, had a lot of wild sex, and partied as much as they could.

After being married about a year, they had one of their huge fights. Her husband chased her with a gun and threatened to kill her. While fighting over the gun, the gun discharged, and her husband fell to the floor bleeding. Scared to death, Martha called for help. When the sheriff arrived, he arrested her and took her to jail. Her husband died from the gunshot wound a few hours later. As a result, Martha spent her next seven years in prison. While in prison, she completed three years of college credits.

After prison, Martha got a job and quickly hooked up with a nice guy and had a daughter with him three months before their wedding. While in college finishing her degree, she became bored with her chronically unemployed husband. Martha divorced her second husband, though fortunately kept custody of her daughter.

Husband number three was wealthy, but physically abusive. After she divorced him, Martha started attending Narcotics Anonymous and Sex and Love Addicts Anonymous. Since that time, she relapsed two times, but had been clean for three years.

"I met Sam at Sex and Love Addicts Anonymous. I know we broke the rules by hooking up with each other, but it has been good for us. Hey, I've been talking about all my trash. Sam, why don't you tell the counselor about your stuff?"

DYSFUNCTION TO THE EXTREME

Sam's marriages had not been as volatile as Martha's, but they were extremely dysfunctional. His outlets were alcohol abuse, strip clubs, and porn. Eventually, he started going to AA and SLAA, where he met Martha.

Martha and Sam's brief courtship had been a whirlwind of passionate sex and yelling matches with some patches of calm. Much of their past experiences, raw emotions, and dysfunctional relationships were on the front burner most of the time. His "insane insecurity" and her "nobody can tell me what to do" attitude led to a stormy, roller coaster relationship.

Sam's frequent accusation to Martha was, "When you're a few minutes late coming home from one of your meetings, I just imagine that you're out there doing your thing with three or four men. I know how you are."

Martha's retort was, "I may have a wild history, but no man is going to take away what I've worked so hard to make of myself. You're just insanely insecure."

WHAT WERE THEY LIKE AS LITTLE KIDS?

While I used about every tool in my therapist's toolbox with Sam and Martha, a significant shift occurred when I asked each of them to sit quietly for five minutes and to imagine what the other was like as a little kid. During those minutes they were very reflective, and their facial expressions softened.

Martha spoke first. "Sam, I think you missed having your dad after your parents divorced when you were six. I know your dad was an alcoholic and ran around on your mom, but I think you missed having a daddy. And I think you felt you had to be the perfect little boy while your mom was off working two jobs to support you all. She's a real piece of work. One minute she's like sticky syrup and the next she's as distant as they come. I think you just wanted to feel loved."

FROM ANGER TO EMPATHY

Martha gently reached out and caressed his arm and

hand. Sam had tears in his eyes. They smiled at each other.

"Oh, little Marty," Sam said tenderly. "You were this cute and feisty little red head. I know that your brother, who was eleven years older, molested you. You kept the secret. That must have been horrible for you. I know you were always smart in school and that your parents only had a sixth-grade education and that you sometimes barely had enough to eat. Your dad was this abusive alcoholic. I'm sure you felt lonely and scared."

Sam reached over and held his wife. They held each other for several minutes. Then Martha said with a smile, "That's the longest we've ever held each other without getting it on." They both laughed, and Sam said, "Maybe we can do this more."

TERMS OF ENDEARMENT

They started calling each other "Sammy" and "Marty." These "names of endearment" led to a lot of loving hugs.

THE TURNING POINT

The turning point for Sam and Martha began with their thinking about the other as an abused or neglected child...or simply as a dear child or person. They began to move from their angry survival modes to empathy and compassion for the other. They looked at each other through compassionate eyes and touched and spoke to each other in a tender manner. This tenderness was anchored every time they spoke to each other by their names of endearment.

THE POWER OF PRAYER

They committed to pray for each other and with each other every day while they held hands. This was another bonding time for them. "It's a lot easier to be kind and considerate to each other since we started praying together," they said.

HEALING AND RECOVERING

Week by week, we went deeper into wounds that needed to be healed and identified loving "gifts" of verbal encouragement or thoughtful acts to give each other. Their road to recovery was often very rough, but they were determined. They continued to go to their Twelve Step meetings. They became active in a Sunday school class at the church where they married. They prayed with each other every day. They continued in therapy with me for over a year and then had "check-up" sessions every couple of months for a while. After moving out of the state, they continued to keep in touch.

DAILY COMMITMENT

Sammy and Marty are still together. Theirs may not be the model marriage for everyone, but it is the best marriage they have ever had. It is amazing what people can do when they really commit to doing everything within their power to make their relationship better.

I sometimes tell this story to couples in my office to give them some perspective of what people in bad marriages can do with strong commitment to make their marriage better and develop genuine compassion for their mates. This is a marriage many people would say did not have a chance to survive, but they worked equally hard as individuals and as a couple to create a good marriage one day at a time, every day, and it worked.

WORDS TO LIVE BY

"We do pray for mercy; and that same prayer teaches us to render deeds of mercy." William Shakespeare

"If you want others to be happy, practice compassion. If you want to be happy, practice compassion." Dalai Lama

FOR PERSONAL REFLECTION:

- How can this story be helpful to you?
- What can help to increase empathy and compassion?

For more questions see the Study Guide in the back of the book.

I May Have Caused My Dad's Death

Grief can be hard enough, but when it is accompanied by guilt, the effects are compounded. What can help our deep feelings of guilt? This story tells about the redemptive power of love and forgiveness.

GRIEF AND GUILT

"I feel so guilty. I think I may have caused my dad's death," said a deeply grieving twenty-year-old Lindsay four weeks after her dad's death. Lindsay explained that she was the rebel of the family while her older brother was the perfect child who did everything right, always graduated at the top of his class, and now had a great job. She, on the other hand, had a higher IQ than her brother, but liked to party. After her dad's death, her mother had screamed at her that she had put her daddy in his grave.

After sobbing for a couple of minutes, Lindsay blew her nose, looked at me with reddened eyes, and said, "I'm a mess."

Lindsay described her dad as a good man, sort of old-fashioned, and a hard-working CPA. She said that she and her dad were close during her growing up years, but the last couple of years had been difficult when she was becoming more independent and making some bad decisions. "I'm afraid he worried so much about me that I caused him to die before his time."

CAUSE OF DEATH

After I empathized with Lindsay that she felt guilty about her dad's death, I asked her to tell me about her dad's health problems and his cause of death.

Lindsay said that her overweight dad had heart problems for several years and died of a heart attack. He was fifty-four years-old at the time of his death, and his dad died of a heart attack at forty-nine. "My mom was always on his case about not taking care of himself and for working too much. She told him many times that he was killing himself."

A DEEPER AWARENESS

At this point, Lindsay paused and looked at me with a quizzical expression. I remained silent and probably raised my eyebrows. Sometimes, caring silence allows a person to gain awareness or insights that have been tucked away until time or space make room for them to emerge. Following this time of silence, I asked Lindsay what she was thinking.

> "I may have been the straw that broke the camel's back, but I think there were several factors that led to my daddy's death. I miss him so much and I carry this heavy guilt inside. I just wish I could tell him that I loved him so much and that I am so sorry for frustrating him and worrying him so much."

THE EMPTY CHAIR CONVERSATION

When I asked Lindsay to describe what her dad looked like, she gave a detailed description of his size, receding hairline, facial features, and his clothing.

Then I told Lindsay I wanted her to imagine her dad sitting in the empty chair and tell him what she wanted to express to him. This invitation gave Lindsay the opportunity to express the feelings she held inside.

Lindsay looked at the empty chair, imagined her dad sitting there, took a deep breath, and began to speak.

"Daddy, I love you so much. You've been a good dad to me all these years. I remember so many good times we had together. We did these math puzzles together and you came to all my piano recitals. I miss you so much. I'm so sorry for worrying you when I stayed out late or didn't even come home. I dated that guy that you knew was not good for me and I drank way too much. I'm so sorry. I don't stay out late anymore. I'm not even dating anyone now. No alcohol for the past three weeks. I love you so much."

I asked her what her dad would say to her. Lindsay thought for a few moments and continued to look at the image of her dad.

"He would say that he loves me. He was a very forgiving man. He would say that he forgives me. He would tell me that I did not cause him to die. He might say that I caused him to lose some of his hair. He'd smile at me. We had this little thing we would do that was like our private code...like when Mom was on the warpath. We'd wink at each other. We are winking at each other now." (Smile)

"Wow! That was kind of strange, but it was wonderful at the same time. I think Mom was in so much pain when Daddy died that she lashed out at me. This is very hard for her. She said she'd like to come in and talk with you, too. I feel this deep and painful emptiness inside, but the huge guilt I felt inside is less now. It was good to have this talk with my daddy. I think I'll have some more conversations with him."

Lindsay continued to have "conversations" with her dad. They helped her to feel a loving closeness again and to feel less guilty.

HEALING

This story is an example of the pain of grief and guilt and what people may feel, say or do in the midst of great loss. Sharing the pain of grief with a trusted friend, family member, clergy person, or counselor can be very helpful. In this process, one can gain awareness, like Lindsay did, that she really did not cause her dad's death.

I think there is bad guilt and good guilt. Some people have what I call "overactive guilt glands." They feel guilt about everything and are controlled by their guilt. Lindsay's guilt was different. She had a "situational" guilt that was a part of her grief. Good guilt can promote change. Confessing her regret to her dad and experiencing his forgiveness helped Lindsay to heal from the pain of her guilt and to make some positive changes in her life.

WORDS TO LIVE BY

"Guilt is perhaps the most painful companion of grief." Coco Chanel

"To err is human; to forgive, divine." Alexander Pope

"Repentant tears wash out the stain of guilt." Saint Augustine

"Forgiveness is the fragrance that the violet sheds on the heel that has crushed it." Mark Twain

FOR PERSONAL REFLECTION:

- How can this story be helpful to you?
- How can talking about a loved one who has died be helpful?

For more questions see the Study Guide in the back of the book.

The Vivid Dream

Have you ever wondered: "What is this dream telling me?" The following dream story may help you look at your own dreams in a meaningful way. This story comes from my second session with Lindsay, whose initial session is recounted in the previous chapter. While Lindsay reported that she was feeling better, that her guilt was lessening, and that she and her mother were having good "heart-to-heart" talks, she was also having "horrible nightmarish dreams."

THE VIVID DREAM

"A couple of nights after Daddy died, I started having this vivid dream. It takes place in our church. The church is filled with people during the worship service. I'm perched on a beam that supports the pitched roof. Below, I see my dad sitting at the end of a pew by the center aisle. My mother is sitting next to him and my brother is sitting next to my mother. I see my dad clutch his chest and almost fall out into the aisle. No one seems to notice, so I swoop down from the ceiling and hold him in my arms. Then, I pick him up and carry him down the center aisle and out of the church. I lay him across the handlebars of my bicycle and I frantically peddle my bike to the hospital. I wake up with this horrible feeling. I don't even want to go to sleep at night because I'm afraid I'll have this dream again. What do you think this means? Can you help me?"

INSIGHT

I asked her what she thought the dream was saying to her.

"Although Dad died in a hospital, the dream takes place in a church. He was a very religious man. He went to church almost every Sunday with my mom and brother. I have not gone to church many times over the past couple of years. Also, in the dream, I'm pretty separated from them…and I was on the ceiling. I've always sort of been off the wall, so those are some of my thoughts."

These were excellent insights into the reason for the setting of the dream and of the family dynamics that included her being more distant or different from her family in recent years. We discussed her unique personality, her relationship with her family, and her thoughts about the church, faith, God, and her dad's death.

FEELINGS

When I asked Lindsay about her feelings in the dream, she said that she did not feel nearly as guilty, but she carried a lot of painful feelings inside. The feelings started when her dad was dying at the hospital. She frantically and helplessly begged the doctors to save her dad's life.

When we hold so many feelings inside, they will come out one way or another. One way is through our dreams.

HOPE

Lindsay and I talked about the stages of grief, and I told her about a conversation I had with Dr. Elisabeth Kubler-Ross, the Swiss-American psychiatrist who pioneered this grief research. Dr. Kubler-Ross said that hope is the final stage of grief. In her heavy accent, she emphasized her words with her curved right index finger,

---

"Hope is always most important...no matter what the situation is. It may not be what you hoped for, or what you thought it should be or wanted it to be. Always look for hope, but it must be realistic hope. Hope is what you will create or what you will create with God's help.

Lindsay said that hope for her would be to have some peace about her dad's death, so, I asked her what she thought would help her experience peace.

PEACE

"The pain of losing him is so deep, but believing that he is at peace helps me. Also, I think that the doctors did everything they could. I held his hand. I'm so glad I was with him and with my mom and brother. I know we loved each other...and that I did not cause him to die. I believe he is at peace. I'll focus on that. This will help me to feel more peaceful. Also, I will remember our wink, and I will continue to have those good conversations with him. It will also help if I don't have those stupid dreams."

I told her to focus on and remind herself of these "peace-givers" every day and that she did not need to have these dreams anymore. I reminded her to keep having good conversations with her dad. She smiled, "Maybe I don't need to have those dreams anymore."

Replacement Dream

When Lindsay came for her next appointment, she beamed: "No more bad dreams." Instead, she had a different dream in which she, her mom, dad, and brother were on a vacation trip. They stopped at a truck stop to eat. When they left the restaurant, her family drove away, and Lindsay left with a truck driver.

Lindsay smiled, "Maybe this is because I had a date for the first time in three months. He's not a truck driver, but he's a good guy I'd like to journey with to see where it goes."

While Lindsay had more grieving and healing to do, this "replacement" dream was a good sign that she was moving on with her life. Dreams can be good indicators of where we are in our lives. After a few more sessions, we concluded her counseling appointments.

ANNIVERSARY REACTION

Several months later I received a phone call from Lindsay. She was perturbed because she had "that stupid dream again."

When Lindsay came for her session, I asked her how long it had been since her dad's death. She said that the prior week had been the one-year anniversary of his death. This is a classic example of what is often called an "anniversary reaction."

MOVING ON

Lindsay and I discussed this common experience of feeling strong emotions around the anniversary of the death of a loved one or of some other painful experience. When I explained that it was "no wonder" she had a recurrence of the dream, she was relieved. It was the last time she had the dream, and Lindsay continued to move on with her life.

BASIC TOOLS TO EXPLORE YOUR DREAMS

Dreams are indicators, guides, or even friends to help you be more aware of what is going on within. Dreams are important for our biological brains and our psychological minds. Address the dream as though you are analyzing a story. Each of the following questions can open the door for insight, descriptions, meaning, and discussion.

1. What is the theme or motif of the dream or series of dreams?

2. What is the setting of the dream?

3. Who are the characters or people in the dream?

4. Are these people you recognize or are they more symbolic figures?

5. If they are known people, how are you similar to or different from them?

6. What are the feelings, emotions, or moods in the dream?

7. What action or movement occurs?

8. What are symbols in the dream?

9. And it is always useful to ask, "What might this dream be telling me?"

WORDS TO LIVE BY

"I dream my painting and I paint my dream." Vincent van Gogh

"I have dreamt in my life dreams that have stayed with me ever after and changed my ideas; they have gone through me, like wine through water, and altered the color of my mind." Emily Bronte

"I love the silent hour of night, for blissful dreams may arise, revealing to my charmed sight what may not bless my waking eyes." Anne Bronte

FOR PERSONAL REFLECTION:

- How can this story be helpful to you?
- What do you think your dreams are telling you?

For more questions see the Study Guide in the back of the book.

Silence

How comfortable are you with silence? For some, silence is uncomfortable or even agonizing. For others, silence is peaceful or golden. I learned the blessing of silence when I frustratingly could not find any words to say to a distressed patient in the hospital.

Dr. Jones said, "Janie is a forty-one-year-old double radical mastectomy patient in 534. As her surgeon, I have done all I can for her. See if you can help her. Good luck!"

This was my third week as a young, inexperienced hospital chaplain intern. I politely thanked the surgeon and nervously walked to Room 534.

"God help me. God help this woman," I prayed.

THE DARK ROOM

Her door was partially open, but the curtains were drawn and her room was dark. I gently knocked on the door and a soft female voice answered, "Who is it?" I said that I was a chaplain. She invited me to come in.

She lay on her back with her eyes closed. I did not want to disturb her, but I said that her surgeon had asked me to visit her. We introduced ourselves and she invited me to sit in a chair close to her bed.

HER DARK STORY

"They had to remove both of my breasts," said Janie. "I really had great breasts. (I blushed.) I feel like I've lost a part of my beauty, my femininity, my sexiness, my womanhood. I wonder if my husband will ever find me desirable again. I've been so depressed. That's probably why Dr. Jones wanted you to visit me."

SWEATY SILENCE

After a few minutes of questions, conversation, and counsel, the verbal exchange halted. She silently stared at the ceiling. I felt very uncomfortable with the silence. Minutes passed.

"God, what should I say," I wondered. This dear woman was going through a horrible experience and I could not think of anything to say. I remembered that agonizing childhood feeling I had at my first (and last) piano recital when my mind blanked. I felt sweaty and anxious.

INSIGHT IN SILENCE

Suddenly, Janie exclaimed, "Do you know what I enjoy doing more than anything else in the whole world? I enjoy dancing more than anything else in the world. While I was lying here, that thought came into my mind. I still hate like the devil that I've lost my breasts, but I just realized that I still have my good legs and feet. When I get better, I'm going dancing."

We smiled at each other. She reached out her hand to me and thanked me. Yet, I had done nothing. At the time, I did not realize it, but that was the best thing I could have done. **Silence.**

THE BLESSING OF SILENCE

In our next two visits, Janie was understandably still feeling depressed and grieving her losses, but her mood improved. A volunteer from an organization that helped people who had mastectomies had met with Janie and given her wise counsel, encouragement and a follow-up plan.

I met Janie's husband just before her discharge from the hospital. "Janie told me about your visits with her," he said. "Thanks for helping her. When she's ready, I'm taking my beautiful wife dancing." They squeezed each other's hands with affection. I did not need to say anything else. In silence, we smiled. He shook my hand and Janie hugged me.

Sometimes, deep feelings can be expressed without saying a word. In crisis, chaos, or everyday life, pausing in silence to simply breathe can relax our bodies and calm our minds. Periods of silence give us the opportunity for the wheels inside our minds to turn without distraction and for us to discover a light bulb of insight or a different perspective. These revelations may gestate for a short or long period of time before they arise.

THE STILL, SMALL VOICE

In quiet times, we can be attuned to the still, small voice inside. Silence allows the internal spirit to move to a deeper level, like the awareness that one can still dance.

WORDS TO LIVE BY

"Learn to get in touch with the silence within yourself." Helen Keller

"Only when you drink from the river of silence shall you indeed sing...then shall you truly dance." Khalil Gibran

---

FOR PERSONAL REFLECTION:

- How can this story be helpful to you?
- How can personal times of silence benefit you?

For more questions see the Study Guide in the back of the book.

Up from the Bathroom Floor

The following story is about using one's own creativity for growth and empowerment.

ABUSIVE MARRIAGE

Jan reported that when she was newly married, she and Pete lived in student housing at college. She vividly remembered lying in the fetal position on the bathroom floor between the commode and the bathtub. Pete stood above her and yelled, "You're a worthless piece of crap!"

This stark scene showed how Jan's marriage began and how it had continued for sixteen years. She looked beaten down as she related a summary of the ups and downs of their marriage.

When I asked Jan what she wanted from therapy, she said that she wanted their marriage to work and for her husband to come with her for the next session.

VOLATILE BEGINNING

Jan and Pete came together to the next appointment. The session began in a seemingly cordial manner as each of them shared some thoughts about their marriage. When

Jan said they had had problems since they were in college, Pete reacted angrily. His face turned beat red. He glared at Jan and forcefully poked his strong index finger into her chest.

I yelled at Pete, "What do you think you are doing!?"

"She made me...!"

"She did not make you do anything! That is physical and emotional abuse and I will not allow it!"

After a few moments of silence, I asked, if this was an example of what went on in their house.

Both responded with a "Sometimes." I felt like a stern parent dealing with an abusive brother hitting his little sister. I took charge of the situation.

No More Abuse

After a few minutes of calmer dialogue, I commanded Pete to commit to not verbally or physically abuse Jan ever again. Although Pete readily agreed, I pressed him until I felt he was committed to our agreement. I knew he needed to address his anger and abusive behavior on a deeper level to protect Jan from his abusive character.

I asked Pete to commit to individual counseling so he would not be abusive to his wife and would be a better role model for their children. Again, he agreed.

Jan watched this process intently. I asked her what she thought about what had just happened. She said she was glad that Pete came to the session and that he would work on his anger that affected her and their children. I asked Jan to counsel with me regarding her issues, and she willingly agreed.

Before they left our session, I once again asked Pete to contract that he would not be physically or verbally abusive to Jan. He looked at Jan and made his verbal commitment. I wanted Jan to feel as safe as she could.

JAN MUST BECOME STRONGER

When I met with Jan at her next appointment, she said she was glad that I had "stood up to Pete." My reaction to Pete was not a sophisticated, premeditated psychological response. It was more of an emergency reaction, but apparently it left a strong impression.

I told Jan that if she chose to stay married to Pete, she would have to be stronger. If she chose to leave him, she would also have to be stronger. I said she must get up from the emotional bathroom floor and be stronger.

"If I get stronger, maybe I won't be so depressed and scared, but I don't think I can stand up to him. I've been in a weak place with him our whole marriage."

Jan reported that she had grown up with a critical and controlling father, so living with an angry and abusive husband was a familiar state. She felt depressed and scared as a child, and she had continued to feel this way in her abusive marriage.

CREATIVE IMAGES

I wondered what Jan had done through the years to survive or what she enjoyed doing. She said that she majored in art and that she really liked being creative and decorating their home.

To use her strength of visual creativity and help her become stronger, I gave Jan a homework assignment. I asked her to develop a clear image of how she wanted to be stronger and a clear image of what her husband was really like.

Jan walked into my office for her next session with a slight smile on her face and brighter eyes. She spoke with a more positive tone and said that she had started her homework by developing a clear image of her husband.

DONALD DUCK

Then Jan posed an amusing question, "Have you ever seen Donald Duck get mad?" I wonderingly said that I had.

"That's my husband! When he gets mad, he flushes red, jumps up and down, and squawks like Donald Duck with his feathers flying." She was right. I had seen it, too. We chuckled and went to work with her image.

When I asked what size her Donald Duck was, I saw Jan look up at the ceiling and her facial expression dropped like I had seen when she came to her initial session. I thought she must be imagining a gigantic Donald Duck staring down at her on the bathroom floor, so, I quickly asked her what size she would like Donald Duck to be. Jan thought for a moment, and with some conviction in her voice, she smiled and said "three-feet short."

ACTION PLAN

Next, we developed an action plan when Pete became angry. She would say to him, "If you can talk with me respectfully, we can talk. If you can't, I'm going to another room, take a walk outside, or drive around the block because I will not allow you to yell at me or abuse me anymore."

That was a big leap for her...empowered strength. She was developing her own sense of being able to stand up for herself as a person with value.

If Pete became angry, Jan would see him as a "three-feet short," squawking Donald Duck with flying feathers. Then, with determination, Jan pointed to her chest and said, "It's just feathers coming from him and those feathers will not penetrate me!"

Yes! I then invited her to stand while she repeated those words with more strength. She smiled and said, "No more abuse."

WONDER WOMAN

At the next session, Jan reported that she had an image for her stronger self. This time, she asked, "Have you ever seen Wonder Woman?" I said, "Yes. She is certainly the image of empowered strength."

"I want to be strong like her. She is beautiful, has a great figure, and she is strong."

Again, we went to work with her image. She described Wonder Woman as strong, with bracelets on her wrists to keep bullets from hitting her and wearing a crown on her head. Jan decided that if her husband became angry, she would imagine him as the little Donald Duck.

She would stand up strong like Wonder Woman, take a good deep breath, exhale slowly, and touch her wrist to remind her that his "feathers" would not penetrate her. She would brush back the front of her hair where a crown would be on her head. She would then say to herself, **"I've been crowned by God and nobody is stronger than God!"**

I wanted Jan to rehearse being Wonder Woman, so she could stand strong. After rehearsing this process a few times, Jan personified empowerment. This strength helped her effectively deal with her husband and their situation.

48

DIVORCE

Pete never laid another finger on Jan and he addressed his anger issues. He eventually confessed to Jan about his year-long affair and told her that he wanted a divorce. Jan said that she had suspected for a long time that he was having an affair, but she had been too afraid to say anything about it. With her new-found strength, she declared that she was going to make it.

Jan and Pete grieved their "failed" marriage, agreed about dealings with their children, worked through an amicable divorce, and moved on with their lives. I also counseled with their children and with them as a family through this process.

EMPOWERED

Jan's strength had grown, and she built a meaningful life for herself and with her children. From her bathroom floor existence, Jan became an empowered Wonder Woman. These two images of Donald Duck and Wonder Woman were representative of and crucial for Jan's growth and strength. I frequently called her "Wonder Woman," and she'd stand straight and strong and we'd smile.

I love counseling with people who can use their own thoughts, creativity, and imagination as tools for their growth and empowerment. When it is their idea or image, they are often more invested in their own therapeutic process and confident in their ability to overcome their problems.

I have shared this story with many people so they can create their own images of strength or ducks. After hearing the story, one abused woman brought two Wonder Woman buttons to her next appointment. She wore one and gave the other to me. I have it on a shelf in my office, and I show it to women who need help feeling empowered.

WORDS TO LIVE BY

"It took me quite a long time to develop a voice, and now that I have it, I am not going to be silent." Madeleine Albright

"No one can make you feel inferior without your consent." Eleanor Roosevelt

"A lot of people are afraid to say what they want. That's why they don't get what they want." Madonna

"Be strong and courageous. Do not fear or be in dread, for it is God who goes with you. God will not leave you or forsake you." Deuteronomy 31:6

"Above all, be the heroine of your life, not the victim. Nora Ephron

---

FOR PERSONAL REFLECTION:

- How can this story be helpful to you?
- How do you want to be more empowered?

For more questions see the Study Guide in the back of the book.

Suicide Prevention

Many people have had suicidal thoughts. What causes some people to not only have suicidal thoughts, but to have a plan? This serious subject is important for all of us to understand as best we can to prevent suicide.

THE FIRST TEARDROP

Eighteen-year-old Jamie walked cautiously into my office wearing a totally black Goth outfit, dark eye-makeup, skull rings on all her fingers, bright green hair, and a red teardrop painted under her right eye. She spoke softly, smiled nervously, and seemed a little spacey. I wondered if she was stoned.

Jamie sat quietly and carefully scanned my whole office. She gave brief answers to my questions and stated that she really did not have any problems, but her mother had made her come to counseling.

Eventually, Jamie revealed that she really missed her brother who had moved away to attend college out of state. "I could always talk to him. He looked out for me. Since he is only one year older, we've always been close. His friends were my friends and we hung out together. After he and his friends left for college, things changed." We talked about this loss, how much she missed her brother, how sad she felt, and how her life had changed.

When I asked Jamie about her red teardrop, she explained that it was her way of expressing her sadness about her best male friend, who had died in a car wreck three months earlier.

"Ethan was a really good guy. He was kind and thoughtful. He never did drugs. He was always the designated driver. It's just not fair that he had to die. I don't really cry or express much emotion. I keep most of it inside."

She denied that she drank or did any drugs, but she did reveal that she had carved "God is Dead" on her upper chest after her friend's death.

"I think that's enough for today," she said.

A NO SUICIDE CONTRACT

I affirmed her pain and told her I appreciated what she had shared with me, but because of her cutting, I was concerned about her potential for further self-harm. I raised my concern with her and after several minutes of discussion, she assured me that she would not harm or kill herself. She wrote a contract that she would not harm or kill herself and committed to bring her parents with her for her next appointment four days later.

True to her word, Jamie brought her parents to her next appointment. Her mom and dad were conservatively dressed and cordial, but they seemed only minimally concerned about their daughter's emotional state. We decided they would sit in the waiting room, and that I'd talk with them following Jamie's session.

Jamie reported that she had been a good kid, made excellent grades, and played high-level soccer. After her brother left, Jamie started hanging out with "different kind of friends." She revealed that she often left school early and smoked weed with her friends.

"Okay, I do some drugs…and yes, when I was here a few days ago, I had smoked some weed before I came. Could you tell?"

I said that I thought she had and that I appreciated her honesty.

"When Ethan was killed, I did not care about anything. I just did more drugs and got more depressed. After he died, I gave up on God. That's when I carved these words on my chest. It hurt so much when he died. He was almost like my brother." A real tear formed in her eye.

When I asked Jamie how depressed she got, she paused and said, "Pretty damn depressed."

I said that I knew she must have so much pain inside to have carved "God is Dead" on her chest. I asked her to tell me how depressed she felt on a scale of zero to ten. "If ten means you feel good and zero means you want to die, where would you say you are on that scale?" She said it was "about a one." Then, I asked her if she thought about hurting herself more or even killing herself.

Jamie sat very still for at least a minute, looked me in the eye, and nodded her head. I leaned forward from my chair and held her hand. She whispered, "I think about it every day. I don't want to hurt my parents or my brother, but the only way I can dull the pain is to drink and do more drugs."

SUICIDE PLAN

I asked if she had a plan to kill herself. She nodded again.

"I would just take an overdose when no one would know...when my parents are at work...in my car...like next week when we're out of school for a day while the teachers have in-service training."

KEEP HER SAFE

A lot was going on in my mind about how suicidal Jamie was. I held both of her hands. We looked at each other and tears were flowing down her cheeks. I told her I could only imagine how much pain she was going through, that I cared for her, and that I would help her stay safe. I also said that we needed her parents' help in this situation.

Jamie did not want her parents to know. I insisted that for her life's sake, she must tell her parents. If she would not, I would because I cared about her and that it was my professional responsibility to tell them so she could get the help she needed.

This is one of those tough situations, but a counselor or anyone else is ethically obligated to do what it takes to protect the person from harming or killing herself. I had staff privileges at a good psychiatric hospital, and I knew that was where Jamie needed to be.

Jamie's parents were unaware or in denial of her deep depression and drug and alcohol abuse. When Jamie shared her feelings and suicide plan with them, they were stunned.

Her dad said, "She just needs to get back in soccer." When I explained the seriousness of Jamie's condition, they began to grasp how critical the situation was...that she could kill herself!

When I told Jamie that she needed to be evaluated at the psychiatric hospital, she bolted out of her chair to leave. I stood in front of my office door to keep her from exiting. Then I told her that it was no wonder she was upset about this, but I cared enough about her, and that her parents cared enough about her to get her to a safe place where she would receive help. This was the best thing we could do for her whether she thought so or not at this time.

Very begrudgingly, Jamie went to the hospital with her parents. She was evaluated and admitted as an in-patient.

FROM ANGER TO APPRECIATION

When I had my initial visit with Jamie at the hospital, she said, "You made me come to this horrible psych hospital." Jamie was furious with me. I visited and counseled with her each day and worked with her team of doctors and nurses. Slowly, Jamie warmed up.

"This is what I needed. I really did plan to kill myself. I was so mad at you, but I thank you."

Testing revealed that Jamie's IQ had dropped from 142 to a little over 100. This is one example of the effect (temporary in her case) that severe depression and drug and alcohol abuse can have on a person. Eventually, Jamie's bright, engaging, and playful personality began to emerge.

I will never forget the night of her prom. Her mom, nurses, and some patients gathered around Jamie to fix her now natural brown hair, and to get her ready for her date to pick her up. We all waved to her as she left the hospital on a pass (until 10 PM) to enjoy her prom. She had a good time and was back on time.

No more alcohol or drugs

A week later, Jamie was discharged from the hospital. In a meeting with her parents in my office, Jamie told her parents how much she loved them and appreciated them.

"None of this was your fault. You may have been naïve and clueless, but you never forced me to take drugs. I take complete responsibility for what I've done. I'm not depressed any more. and I'm not going to drink alcohol or do drugs. I will continue to counsel with Dr. Parsons and I will attend AA meetings five times a week. I'm going to be okay. In fact, I'm better than I've been in a long time."

Her bright smile and sparkling eyes spoke volumes.

Jamie kept her commitments. As the red carving of "God is Dead" on her chest healed, she even "patched up" her relationship with God. Her brother came home for the summer and they reconnected in a meaningful way.

Jamie went out of state to college, remained active in AA, graduated in three and one-half years with a degree in secondary education and volunteered to speak to some of my counseling classes at SMU.

If you would like more information about suicide prevention, you can find that information online, in resource material and books, from qualified professionals, or from suicide prevention hotlines. Some basic information about suicide prevention can be found in the Study Guide in the back of the book.

WORDS TO LIVE BY

"When you feel like giving up, just remember the reason why you held on for so long." Unknown

"There is help. There is hope. You are not alone." Suicide Prevention Awareness

---

FOR PERSONAL REFLECTION:

- How can this story be helpful to you?
- What will help you not to harm or kill yourself?

For more questions see the Study Guide in the back of the book.

Do you carry around a lot of painful feelings? Most of us do. We benefit from being able to release these feelings, so they won't cause "emotional constipation." Following is the story about a boy with a lot of painful feelings who found a creative outlet.

PULLED APART BY PARENTS

Ten-year-old James was a bright, precocious, and good-looking only child whose parents were pulling him apart as they divorced and pressured him to pick his favorite parent. He said, "This drives me crazy!" James expressed how much he loved both his parents and that he did not want them to divorce. "If they see how hard this is for me, maybe they won't get a divorce."

He shed a few tears and said in a resigned voice, "They tell me that I just have to accept the fact that they are divorcing. I know they love me, but it hurts so much." We both shook our heads with a mutual understanding of the inevitable. It was sad, but James said, "I'm glad you understand this is so hard for me."

TAKE NOTES

My second meeting with James was very engaging. We

talked about his interests, his friends, his family, and his feelings. At the end of the session, James commented, "I noticed that you did not take any notes during our session today like you did last time." I responded that I would make some notes later. He seemed disappointed, so I asked him if he would like for me to take notes during our meetings. He replied, "Yes, I would. You see, when you take notes, I think that what I'm saying to you is important." So, I took some notes during our next sessions. James was telling me that he wanted to be heard and that his words were valued.

A Bundle of Feelings

James was a straight-A student at an excellent private school. He also took trumpet lessons. His outward appearance looked like he had everything under control, but inside, James carried a bundle of feelings: sad, depressed, scared, worried, and angry. When I asked him what he did with all these feelings, he said, "I think I take them out on my trumpet teacher. If he's not paying attention to me, I turn my trumpet toward him and BLAST him!"

We laughed and concluded that there might be a better way to let go of his feelings. He said he could express his feelings in our sessions, but he needed a way to let go of his feelings when he was home. We explored some options. Telling his parents? "I'm not ready to do that yet." he replied. Hitting his bed or pillow? "That doesn't seem quite right."

Kick out the emotions

Suddenly, the light bulb went off for James: "I'd rather kick!" Since kicking is an even more visceral and powerful way to physically release emotions, this seemed like a great choice. We brainstormed what he could kick that would not damage property, other people, or his own feet. Finally, we came up with the idea that cardboard boxes would do the trick. He could keep a couple of them in his room and a few extras in the garage. James confirmed this decision with a litany of benefits of kicking cardboard boxes: "I can kick them as hard as I want. It will make some noise, but not too much noise. My foot won't get hurt because I'll only kick with my shoes on. And it will feel good to just kick out my feelings. I probably did that when I was a little kid and threw temper tantrums."

THE SOLUTION

James was very satisfied with this solution. He smiled, "My trumpet teacher will probably like it, too." We laughed. Then James said, "Hey! I know where the best boxes are...the liquor store!" When his mother came to pick up James after the session, I told her I wanted her to go by the liquor store and that James would tell her the reason. James grinned. She seemed a little puzzled, but it was certainly a familiar store for her and James' dad.

James kicked a lot of boxes over the next several weeks. I counseled with James, with his parents, and with them as a family as they dealt with feelings, made decisions, and worked out plans to create the best conditions they could for James' well-being. His parents chuckled, "We've even kicked the boxes a few times ourselves."

THE REST OF THE STORY

Several years later I received a handwritten note from James saying that he was graduating from college and would be entering medical school in the fall. Way to go James!

LETTING GO

When we hold painful feelings inside, we can become depressed or stuck in an unhealthy state. To progress emotionally, we must let go of the "emotional constipation" that blocks our moving on with our lives.

How can we release our feelings? We can talk them out with a friend or professional. We can write them, so they don't stay in our minds. We can calm them by breathing or meditating. We can use a cognitive tool of identifying the feelings and negative thoughts and replacing them with rational thoughts. We can exercise or engage in physical activities. We can imagine them as concrete objects and let them go. We can hit pillows... or kick cardboard boxes.

WORDS TO LIVE BY

One Definition of Kick: "to free oneself of something."

"Anger is fuel. We feel it and we want to do something...throw a fit...Anger is a voice, a shout, a plea, a demand...With a little thought, we can usually translate the message that our anger is sending us." Julia Cameron, The Artist's Way

---

FOR PERSONAL REFLECTION:

- How can this story be helpful to you?
- How do you deal with stored feelings?

For more questions see the Study Guide in the back of the book.

When someone commits suicide, their loved ones are left with a traumatizing grief, among other emotions. While this will not be a pleasant story for you to read, I hope it will be helpful to you personally or with people you know and that it can give you hope.

WE NEED YOUR HELP

"We need your help. My husband committed suicide two weeks ago. We found him hanging in the garage. My children and I really need help." These desperate and haunting words were my introduction to Phyllis in her initial phone call to me.

HORRIBLY SAD AND SEVERELY DEPRESSED

The next day, she and her children, thirteen-year-old Frank and eight-year-old Courtney, walked somberly into my office. Phyllis shared that her husband, Clark, had bouts of severe depression for many years and had been under the care of a psychiatrist for most of that time.

She explained that Clark had a raging type of depression. Over the years she had taken her children to a neighbor's house or to a hotel when he would have one of his violent episodes. By the time they returned the next day, he'd be subdued. This time, he was shaking the refrigerator and screaming. Almost like having a fire escape plan, she took Frank and Courtney to a hotel for the night. When they returned, they found Clark...he was hanging in the garage. As she said these painful words, they all looked so horribly sad.

Phyllis said that since Clark's funeral ten days earlier, Frank had punched holes in the wall and Courtney had clung to her day and night. Phyllis had focused on the care of her children and the necessary arrangements and decisions about the funeral and Clark's business. The combination of grief, trauma from seeing the suicidal hanging, and years of emotional struggle had left this family in a severely depressive state.

FRANK'S STORY: SO DAMN HORRIBLE

Frank looked at me with a traumatized expression and cried, "It was so damn horrible." Then, gritting his teeth and pounding his fists up and down on the arms of the chair, "How could he do that," he screamed. In the early sessions, Frank expressed his anger, frustration, fears, traumatized emotional pain, sadness, and grief. We found two ways that were most helpful for Frank to release his emotions. One was to pace around my office and yell, scream, cry, and talk about and express his pain. The other was to go to the batting cage and pound out his feelings on baseballs. This also improved his batting skills.

LOVE-HATE RELATIONSHIP

Frank described the love-hate relationship he had with his dad. He said his dad could be good when he talked with him about his schoolwork, when they talked about the Yankees, or played catch. When they lived in New Jersey before they moved to the Dallas area five years earlier, his dad took him to some Yankee games. But Frank's dad could be a monster. Something would set him off and he'd go ballistic. "I just hated that," Frank said. Then, Frank talked about "the horrible day." With long pauses and bitterly hot tears, Frank told the story. "We came home from the hotel about ten o'clock on Saturday morning. As the garage door went up, there he was. He was just hanging in the garage."

TENDERNESS AND LOVE

Eventually, Frank felt and expressed the tenderness and love he held in his heart for his dad. One day I asked Frank if he'd like to write a letter to his dad. In fact, he wrote several letters expressing his painful feelings, memories, and love. In a final "good-bye" letter, he recalled the good times they had at Yankee Stadium, and stated that one day in the future, he would go back there "for old times' sake."

Over time, Frank transformed his wall-punching anger into being the best home run hitter on his baseball team. His coach took Frank under his wing and became a good male role model and confidant for Frank. In this process, Frank let go of "the horrible day" image of his dad hanging in the garage and replaced it with images of the two of them happily playing catch in the backyard.

COURTNEY'S STORY: VERY SAD

Courtney had a very close relationship with her mother

because her dad's mood swings and volatile behaviors scared her. In her quiet voice she said, "I'm very sad. I think Daddy was very sick and he couldn't get better. When I saw my daddy's feet that day in the garage, I just hid my eyes and held onto my mommy. I cry and I pray. I think my daddy loved me a lot and I loved him…and I always will."

Phyllis was very comforting and even protective of her daughter. Courtney said she liked to draw, so I asked her to draw pictures of anything she wanted. She drew pictures of her family, her dad, herself, and her feelings. "I feel better when I draw pictures. I like to color them, too. Mommy said it would be okay for me to put them on the walls of my room. I like that." During the therapy process, her pictures illustrated her emotional movement. The pictures became brighter, and the expressions of her dad moved from sad or angry to a picture of him smiling in heaven.

SUMMER CAMP

That summer, Courtney who'd just turned nine, had the opportunity to attend a week-long camp. I discussed this with Phyllis and Courtney. Will she feel secure enough to be away that long? Will she become depressed? Phyllis talked with the camp leaders about Courtney's dad's suicide. The camp would start three and a half months after his death. Courtney's two best friends were also going to the camp. We all concluded this could be a positive experience for her.

When she returned from camp, Courtney said she had some sad feelings during the first days away from home, but she reported having "a really good time. I even did things I'd been afraid to do before. I rode a horse. I really liked doing that every day. One night at the campfire, I led a song in front of everybody. And my drawing about my favorite thing at camp won first prize. I drew a picture of me riding my horse." Courtney and Phyllis smiled and hugged. The camp experience proved to be a turning point for Courtney. When she returned, she smiled more, was more confident, and less clingy to her mother. She also started taking horseback riding lessons.

PHYLLIS' STORY: DEPRESSED AND SURVIVING

While Phyllis focused much of her energy into being a good mom, her own depression was mounting. She had spent so much time over the years managing the roller coaster life with Clark, rearing the children almost totally by herself, and just trying to survive. All of this had taken a tremendous toll on her. Since her husband's traumatizing suicide, Phyllis was depressed.

In an individual session, Phyllis confided, "Sometimes, I don't feel like I can do it anymore. My marriage was hell much of the time and my own dad was a piece of work. I've tried my whole life to do the right thing, but no matter what I do, I've never been good enough. Sometimes I just hate myself. Sometimes I've thought the world would be better off if I'd never been born. I've tried to protect my children, but I could not do enough. They had to see their dad be so horrible and then to have their last image of their dad hanging in the garage. I think they are getting better, but I'm not sure about me."

RELEASE MISERABLE CRAP

We addressed her history of feeling badly about herself

as she dealt with an emotionally abusive dad and a depressive, volatile, and abusive husband. Week after week we focused on her healing and recovering from her own depression and the grief and trauma of her husband's suicide. Expressing her deep and well-guarded emotions allowed Phyllis to release "all this miserable crap I've stuffed inside for years...really for all my life." She also benefitted from writing her feelings, memories, and personal stories in a journal.

KEPT HUSBAND ALIVE AND FAMILY TOGETHER

One day, I asked Phyllis to tell me about how she had tried to help Clark through the years. She described seventeen years of loving him, taking care of him, taking him to appointments with psychiatrists, keeping him from overdosing on his medications, making sure he was taking his medication as prescribed, staying with him through the "horrible times", and praying for him.

When I asked Phyllis how she had tried to be a good mom she said, "They've been my reason for living. I've tried to protect them from all the chaos, but that was impossible. I tell them every day how much I love them. I'm strict about their being honest and doing their schoolwork and chores. I'm there for them in their activities. I take them to Sunday school and church. I pray for them. I guess I've been their constant parent."

A REMARKABLE PERSON

I looked at Phyllis and said that I thought she was a remarkable person and that I could only imagine how hard it had been through all these years, and through Clark's suicide. I told her that she had done an amazing job, that I admired how much she had done for her husband, and that she had saved his life many times. I shared what a wonderful mom she was, and I restated that I thought she was a remarkable person.

Phyllis listened carefully to what I said as she rubbed her bare upper arms. I said gently, "Look at your hands and arms. What are you doing?" She looked down and saw her hands caressing her arms.

Simultaneously, tears leapt from her eyes and goose bumps sprang up on her arms as she exclaimed, "I'm loving myself! My God, for the first time in my life, I'm actually loving myself!"

We smiled at each other with tears in our eyes. Phyllis finally whispered with an expression of amazement, "I guess this is what I've wanted all my life. Thank you."

PROFOUND TRANSFORMATION

Later, she explained that this profound transformation was a physical, emotional, and spiritual awakening of love for herself, that until then had only been an intellectual concept. "Through all of the abuse growing up and Clark's depression and suicide, I just didn't think it was possible."

While she had many challenging days ahead of her, that powerful and unforgettable experience of loving herself helped Phyllis move toward healing and gaining confidence in herself. She loved others deeply, and now, she could love herself, too. Lovingly caressing her arms became a daily ritual that helped her healing.

PRAYERS AND HUGS

Phyllis, Frank, and Courtney continued to heal and

grow individually and as a family. They developed a new ritual of family prayer that concluded with a family hug. Frank no longer put holes in the wall.

BASEBALL

Playing baseball became his passion. When he hit home runs, he used the ritual of pointing to his dad in heaven as he circled the bases. His baseball coach helped him tape, bed, and paint over the holes he'd punched in the walls. He also helped to fill Frank's emotional holes by being a good man Frank could look up to.

DRAWING, HORSEBACK RIDING, CHOIR

With less chaos in the family, Courtney felt more secure and blossomed into a more verbally expressive person. Drawing, horseback riding, and an engaging social life helped Courtney feel happy again. She also started singing in her church's children's choir.

TURNING TRAGEDY INTO HELPING OTHERS

I encouraged Phyllis to attend a Survivors of Suicide support group. This caring group of people with similar experiences helped her know she "was not the only one who was a survivor of suicide." I also supported Phyllis' return to college to complete the six hours for graduation. Her major paper was about "Survivors of Suicide." The paper was so extraordinary that her professor submitted it for a congressional hearing on suicide. Phyllis went to Washington D. C. and gave a presentation about survivors of suicide. Phyllis said, "Out of this horrible experience that devastated us, I hope my paper will help people in powerful positions in our government to know what a huge issue suicide is and its effects on so many families. Also, I've grown to be a stronger person than I ever thought I could be, and I want to help others who are survivors of suicide."

MOVING ON

While the pain of suicide left a lifetime of haunting images and deep scars of emotions and grief, these survivors diligently worked to heal and move on with their lives as best they could. Anniversaries, Father's Day, Christmas, birthdays, and other reminders were difficult. Each of them vowed to "never ever commit suicide." They also committed to stay "on track about their mental health," and to be aware of any tendency toward depression. They created a family motto: "We love each other and we love ourselves." Phyllis continued to caress her arms on a regular basis as a reminder of, "I love myself."

What remarkable individuals and what a remarkable family! People like Phyllis, Frank, and Courtney inspire me, and I share their lives with the hope that their stories will help others.

WORDS TO LIVE BY

"Allow yourself to grieve. We all grieve in our own time in our own way." Sally Ann Gazner

"A person never truly gets 'over' a suicide loss. You get through it. Day by Day. Sometimes its moment by moment." Holly Kohler

"Please reach out. Speak up. The worst thing you could do is to stay silent, like I did for so many years." Kelsey Elizabeth Oney

"One day you'll wake up and things won't hurt as bad. You'll be able to remember the good things about your loved one and not just the end. For me, that's when I knew I was finally able to move on." Kristin Svinth

"So far, the best thing for me has been advocating during difficult times for prevention. It helps me to focus on the positive." Sherrie Gerdon

FOR PERSONAL REFLECTION:
- How can this story be helpful to you?
- What do you think is helpful for survivors of suicide?

For more questions see the Study Guide in the back of the book.

We Go for the Jugular

We all have arguments and conflict with people in our families. How we deal with past and present problems in our relationships is crucial for our survival and the well-being of those closest to us. The following story of redemptive love gives us hope.

DEVASTATING EXPERIENCES

Russ and Sue's conflict style was: "We go for the jugular!" How did this pleasant appearing couple become so destructively combative and what would help them save their marriage? They had two devastating experiences early in their marriage. Sue had a major depressive episode that involved being hospitalized in a psychiatric unit for three weeks. A few years later, Russ had an extramarital affair that almost ended their marriage.

When they had a disagreement about their children, finances, or something as simple as who should change the cat's litter, they went straight for the emotional vein in the neck that returns blood to the heart from the brain. With lightning fast speed these disagreements escalated to a full blown, jugular-grabbing, frontal attack of cruel judgments about Sue having been in the "nut house" or Russ being a "cheating SOB." They concluded, "If we don't change how we deal with each other, we are going to kill each other and mess up our kids."

EMPATHY AND FORGIVENESS

In our first several sessions, we addressed their wounded feelings, damaged relationship, and alternative ways of dealing with issues. Russ learned more about Sue's depressive experience and really listened to her story of emotional pain and immobilizing depression. He *developed* empathy for and sensitivity to Sue's feelings left over from her dad's affair when she was an adolescent. And, he genuinely apologized for his affair, his insensitivity to her feelings, and his emotional battering of the woman he said he loved so much.

Sue declared that it had been fifteen years since Russ' "two-night stand." She said he had profusely apologized to her many times and she believed he had been faithful to her since that time. Although she had been "torpedoed" by his unfaithfulness, Sue said she needed *"to heal* that deep emotional wound of betrayal, to *really forgive* Russ, and not allow that past event to control her view of herself, her husband, or her marriage." This self-described "survivor" worked hard to heal, forgive, and *let go of* the "painful and vivid memory" of her dad's affair and Russ' infidelity that had so profoundly affected her life and marriage. Still, Russ and Sue would slip and resort to a milder version of their old jugular attacks. Their homework assignment was to identify a way to stop them.

SWEAR ON THE BIBLE

At the beginning of our next session, Russ said he had taken the assignment seriously. He asked if I had a Bible in my office. I replied that I did. Then, he made an offer I had never heard in all my years of counseling. Russ said that he would be willing to swear on the Bible that he would never again raise Sue's depression, or anything related to it, unless she brought it up and wanted to talk about it.

After carefully exploring his readiness to make such a vow, I retrieved a Bible from the shelf. As I did, I heard Sue clear her throat. When I looked at her, she had tears in her eyes. Then she announced that she would also like to put her hand on the Bible and swear to never again throw Russ' infidelity in his face.

HEARTFELT VOWS

The three of us thoroughly discussed the significance of *communicating* these heart-felt vows and the seriousness of the sacred covenant they wanted to make. In a scene that was part swearing-in ceremony, part surrendering their warring swords, part reconciling their relationship, and part renewing their wedding vows, I held the Bible while Russ and Sue lay their hands on it.

Russ and Sue proceeded to speak some of the most powerfully soulful words I have ever witnessed. They included their commitment to lovingly kiss each other's neck every day as a way of sealing their vow. This was "holy ground." They emotionally embraced each other and continued their expressions of apology, forgiveness, promise, and love. Then, they kissed each other's necks, wiped their tears, and smiled.

At a checkup session one year later after their concluding session, Russ and Sue had kept this commitment.

Couples who can listen with empathy, genuinely apologize for their insensitivity, and really forgive each other can experience a deep level of healing in their relationship. When these essential elements are anchored by serious and sacred vows of commitment and daily hugs and kisses, marriage can thrive.

WORDS TO LIVE BY

"Anger is the wind that blows out the candle of the mind." Robert Ingersol

"Understand this, my dear brothers and sisters: You must all be quick to listen, slow to speak, and slow to get angry." James 1:9

FOR PERSONAL REFLECTION:

- How can this story be helpful to you?
- How do you deal with conflict?

For more questions see the Study Guide in the back of the book.

If you've ever experienced a trauma, you know its powerful and lingering effects. The following is one remarkable person's story of trauma and healing.

DINA'S STORY

"My dad raped me." Dina was nineteen-years-old and spoke in brief, shock-like sentences. She had a frightened expression in her eyes, and she whispered her story.

"When I was a little girl – from about five until I was nine – my dad and granddad molested me." She told her mother, but her mother did not believe her. Then, she told the minister. She thought "this man of God" would surely believe her and help her. The minister said that her daddy and granddaddy were deacons in the church, and they would never do anything like that. He told her to never let him hear her say anything about this again, so, Dina kept it secret. After her granddad died, she told her teacher at school. The teacher believed her and reported it to CPS. There was a trial and her dad went to prison.

Dina looked at me with a pained expression and continued.

"I had not seen my dad in all of these years until he came to my apartment three days ago. He knocked on my door, told me he was my dad, and that he wanted to talk to me. So many thoughts raced through my mind, but I thought that maybe he had changed and that we could talk. I let him in. We sat and talked for a few minutes. Then he stood up and tried to hug me. I did not want that. He grabbed me and forced me onto the floor. I tried to push him away and I yelled at him to leave me alone. He is so big and strong. He held me down...and my dad raped me," she wailed. "I reached for a lamp behind me to hit him. He finally left. I was so messed up. I did not know what to do. So, I called my neighbor who called the police and took me to the hospital."

RECURRING DREAM

During the ensuing weeks, as Dina dealt with the trauma of her rape and other family issues, she had a recurring dream that reenacted the rape experience. The dream always ended with Dina reaching for the lamp to hit her dad while simultaneously thinking, "But I can't hit him. He's my dad."

This dream captured Dina's internal conflict about her dad. "I'm afraid of going to sleep because I'll have this horrible dream again. I've got to get rid of this dream."

Of course, this nightmare was the result of her traumatic experience. While it was completely understandable for Dina to have this recurring dream, she said, "It's like the dream controls and abuses me like my dad did."

TAKING CHARGE

I asked Dina, "If you could take charge of your dream and control how it goes, how would you change it?" Dina paused and thought for a few moments. The question helped shift her attention from emotional pain to rational thinking about how she could change the dream.

Dina related that she may not have been able to keep her dad from coming to her apartment, but she would not let him enter. "When I hear my dad knock at the door, I will not let him in. Instead, I'll imagine putting three big locks on the door."

This sounded like a good plan. We rehearsed the scene several times with Dina speaking louder and stronger each time. "Go away! I will not allow you to come in! Go away!" She said she would do this several times before she went to bed each night.

At her next appointment, Dina reported that she continued to have the same horrible dream and was not sleeping well. I wondered if this was going to be an effective method for Dina. I asked her if she wanted to try again. She did.

We rehearsed the dream again. Dina stood at my office door and described the scenario. "I hear my dad knock at the door. I put three big locks on the door...and (*with a powerful lifting motion*) I place this four-foot long heavy iron bar across the door. 'Go away! I will not let you in! Go away!' My dad pounds on the door and finally walks away." She repeated this script many times with strength and determination. Again, she committed to do this exercise each night.

At our next session, Dina was smiling.

> *"I did it! I did it just like we did it here. My dad knocked on the door. I placed the locks on the door and the big iron bar across the door. He knocked and knocked. I yelled at him to go away. Finally, I heard his footsteps walking away from my apartment door and down the steps. I heard him get in his car and drive away. I've had this new dream three times in the past week. I did not have that bad dream once. Last night, I just had a good and peaceful sleep.*

TURNING POINT

This was a turning point for Dina. She continued to make good progress as she healed from the childhood molestation, the betrayal from her mother and minister, and the rape. Dina also ended a relationship with a not-so-good boyfriend and began to feel freer and stronger than ever before.

Dina testified at her dad's trial with determined strength. Her dad went back to prison for life.

STEPS TO HEALING

Seek help.

Dina called a neighbor who took her to the hospital. The doctor referred her to me, and the neighbor brought her to her first appointment.

Have a safe placed to share your story.

Dina said, "If I start talking, my stuff may splatter all over the walls." I assured her that she could express everything she wanted." She did.

Address the issue you think is most crucial.
Dina wanted to address the nightmarish dream, so she could sleep.
Move from the victim state to being emotionally stronger.
Dina began this process when she shifted from the emotional pain she was feeling, to rational thinking about what she could do.
Take charge of your life.
Dina courageously addressed the painful wounds of the past and present and she took on the persistent power to change her dream and take charge of her life.

A LEARNING EXPERIENCE

Of course, deep memories and scars remain, but these are some of the keys to healing from trauma. This was one of my first experiences as a counselor after leaving hospital chaplaincy. I conferred with a seasoned therapist to help me effectively counsel Dina. I cared about her as a person, thought what would be helpful, and tried to do the best I could as her counselor. I learned a lot from this remarkable and courageous young woman.

WORDS TO LIVE BY

"Trauma is personal. It does not disappear if it is not validated. When it is ignored or invalidated, the silent screams continue internally heard only by the one held captive. When someone enters the pain and hears the screams, healing can begin." Danielle Bernock

"You may not control all the events that happen to you, but you can decide not to be reduced by them." Maya Angelou

FOR PERSONAL REFLECTION:

- How can this story be helpful to you?
- How do you deal with painful memories?

For more questions see the Study Guide in the back of the book.

Anger Management

Do you ever get angry? We all do. How we deal with our anger is crucial for our well-being, and for the well-being of those around us.

ROAD RAGE

He was a tall, slender minor league baseball pitcher with a pulverized face. His nose was smashed and stitched, and his eyes were circled with dark bruises and more stitches. "This is what road rage can get you," Don explained. "I was almost roadkill. I need help."

While driving on an interstate highway, another driver cut in front of Don. This triggered his road rage. After cutting in front of each other a couple of times as they raced down the interstate, the other driver exited to an access road, and Don followed him until they stopped on the gravel shoulder.

Both angry men got out of their cars and the other driver pulled a "huge pistol" and threatened to kill Don. "He aimed the gun at my head. I just prayed and closed my eyes. I thought I was a dead man. Then I felt this horrible crunch between my eyes." When Don came to, a passing motorist was tending to him. He was taken by ambulance to a nearby hospital emergency center. The doctor told him he had not been shot, but the guy had smashed him with a big pistol right between the eyes.

Don looked at me with a pained expression and said, "My nose was crushed and the orbital bones around my eyes were broken. I could have been killed. My doctor told me to come see you, so I don't ever do this again. I don't think I will, but I've got to be sure. So here I am."

WHAT CAUSES SUCH RAGE?

After some questions to determine the scope of Don's anger, we concluded that he only had rage problems when he drove. As we discussed his personality traits and emotional coping mechanisms, Don had a profound realization. The competitive drive that helped him be successful in sports became a fiery, out-of-control competitive drive when he drove his sports car.

"I hate losing. In baseball, I had to learn to control my anger at myself, with opposing hitters, and umpires. In my car, I've not done that. I get uncontrollably angry with other drivers when I feel like I'm losing to them or they're acting stupid."

IDENTIFY EXISTING TOOLS

Making it relatable to his profession, I asked him what he did when he became angry in a game. Don explained that after getting thrown out of a few games earlier in his career, he learned to bark cuss words into his glove. If someone hit a home run, he'd shake his head and shake off his anger and get his head back in the game.

In tense situations during a game, he'd walk around on

the mound, take deep breaths, and calmly talk to himself. He had developed a ritual of rotating the ball in his hand to get a "handle" on his emotions and get the right feel of the ball.

BREATHE AND ROTATE THE BALL

With these coping methods already in place, we talked about how he could apply them on the highway. What if you keep a baseball in your car? If someone cuts you off, you can pick up your friend the baseball and rotate it just like you do on the pitcher's mound. He smiled. "I think that is a great idea." Don decided to keep a baseball in the console of his car. If he felt agitated while driving, he would rotate the ball in his right (pitching) hand and breathe calming breaths. These physical reminders of breathing and a baseball helped him calm his body and "handle" his emotions.

HELPFUL REMINDERS

I asked Don what he said to himself to calm down after he walked a batter or gave up a homerun. He responded that he would take a breath and say to himself, "Okay, you've done this thousands of times. Be calm. Just throw this ball where the catcher is holding his glove," Then he would go into his motion and throw his pitch.

Since his calming self-talk helped Don on the mound, I suggested a simple verbal reminder while in his car. When he put his hands on the steering wheel, he'd take a breath, smile, and say, "I'm thankful to be alive and I will enjoy my drive." We laughed and high fived. Don said, "I'm getting equipped to do away with road rage."

Later, Don's girlfriend gave him a little stuffed raccoon

to remind him of the effects of his road rage. Don hung it from his rear-view mirror. This was a humorous, yet painful reminder of the road rage experience that left him looking like a pulverized raccoon. "Now, when I get in my car, I look at that little guy and say, 'I'm lucky to be alive and I'm going to enjoy my drive'."

PRACTICE, PRACTICE, PRACTICE

Don committed to practice this ritual before he even started the engine. This combination of tools (rotating the baseball in his right hand, taking calming breaths, saying his verbal reminder, and seeing the little stuffed raccoon) helped Don enjoy driving. A key to this athlete's success was knowing the importance of practice. He practiced these reminders every time he got in his car.

While some anger issues require more in-depth analysis and therapy, specific issues like Don's respond well to simple and focused approaches. He enjoyed reporting how he calmly handled potentially triggering driving situations. I determined that he did not have other underlying problems, and he had already learned some effective tools to manage his anger from his baseball experience. I basically drew from this success and helped him to apply similar tools to driving situations.

I played baseball for years and have been a life-long student of the game. This helped me easily relate to Don and "speak his language." The collection of autographed baseballs on a shelf in my office also aided our connection.

Find a good tool that fits you and practice, practice, practice. When you are in one of those triggering situations, you will be equipped to handle your emotions in an effective way.

WORDS TO LIVE BY

"When anger rises, think of the consequences." Confucius
"To be angry is to revenge the faults of others on ourselves."
Alexander Pope

FOR PERSONAL REFLECTION:

- How can this story be helpful to you?
- What tools will help you with your anger?

For more questions see the Study Guide in the back of the book.

So many children are abused, and often when they tell someone, they are not believed. Their courage to survive and eventually get help, let alone share their story is remarkable. This story is about one of those amazing people.

ABUSE

Behind the beautiful blond sorority girl's appearance hid the horrors of abuse. Kim began by saying that she had anxiety issues. "I think I've felt anxious for a long time...since I was a child. It may have something to do with some abuse I experienced during my childhood."

When a person uses the word "abuse," I know it can mean all kinds of cruelty. When the abuse has occurred in childhood, I want to be as gentle as I would be with a child. As a male therapist, I was especially aware of the importance of not only being gentle, but reassuringly strong, to be a safe place and person for this abused young woman to share openly.

PHYSICAL ABUSE

> "After my parents divorced when I was seven, my mother had a relationship with Bob whom she planned to marry. He eventually moved in with us and while my mom worked nights as a nurse, he would abuse me. He shoved me around. He threw me into the wall and knocked me into a chest of drawers. When Mom saw the bruises, he claimed that I was jealous of their relationship and that I would throw myself into the wall, so she would think he was abusing me. My mom believed him. I would tell her, cry to her and beg her, but he was so convincing in what he would say. He was good to my mom, but he hated me."

Kim's pained facial expression and voice projected the horrifying effects of being shoved, thrown and knocked around. Her pain was compounded by the helpless and desperate feelings she had as a child when her mother would not believe her. These experiences of physical abuse were enough to cause her to have post-traumatic effects.

SEXUAL ABUSE

> "But there's more. He would expose himself to me and would tell me that I wanted him and that he would teach me how to treat a man sexually. He'd try to force me to..., but when he did that, I would run to my room and lock the door."

I commended her for being able to escape Bob's attempts to force her into sexual acts. She nodded her head, looked me in the eyes, and continued. "When I was in the third grade, the school counselor came to our classroom and talked about sexual abuse. I went home and told my mom about what Bob was doing, but again, she did not believe me because he was so convincing. He said that I was doing everything I could to break them up. When Mom was around, he was so polite and kind and helpful. He told my mom how much he loved me and that he wanted to become a wonderful step-dad to me."

Eventually, Kim did talk to the school counselor who reported this to CPS. In her case, the CPS investigation did not conclude that there was enough evidence to continue their process, but they told Kim's mom to take Kim to a counselor. Kim said she was hopeful that finally she could get some help, but her mother did not follow through.

SURVIVING ABUSE

Kim concluded that it was useless to try to convince her mom how abusive Bob was because she was so "in love" with him. Kim decided that she had to survive the best way she could by staying in her room and reading when at home and staying with friends as often as possible. Kim made good grades and was popular with her classmates, but she was very anxious about going on dates. If she went on a date, she would not let a boy hold her hand. I told her it was no wonder she felt the way she did.

HE'S DEAD

Then, Kim told me that Bob had died in a car accident three years earlier. I said that I was glad he was no longer a threat to her and glad he was dead. Kim looked a little surprised at my statement. "So, you don't think it's bad for me to secretly be glad he's dead?" "No, I don't. No wonder you would think this. I'm just glad he can't harm you anymore." Kim smiled, "Thank you." she said, "There's more I need to tell you next time."

LIFE-THREATENING ABUSE

At the beginning of our next session, Kim related that it was hard for her to recall these horrible events because she had "stuffed them deep inside." Yet, she said that it helped when she shared the experiences and I listened.

Kim's account of Bob's cruel sociopathic methods finally reached a bone-chilling, life-threatening level.

> "He quit the physical abuse and he knew I would not tolerate his exposing himself to me and trying to force me to do sexual things, so he tried another tactic. He wanted me to kill myself. He looked deep into my eyes in his penetrating and evil way, like he was trying to cast a spell on me. He said, 'I want you to kill yourself. You are keeping your mother from having me to love her and to take care of her, so I want you to plan how you will kill yourself. You will tell me your plan tomorrow, and then the next day you will kill yourself.' I guess he figured if he could get me to kill myself, it would prove to my mom that I was crazy and that he had been right."

THE VOICE INSIDE

Kim said she was scared, but she was determined to survive and not to kill herself. She said she heard a voice in her head—like God saying, "Tell him how you will do it, but don't do it. I am with you." She told Bob that she had a plan. After school the next day, she would jump in front of a big truck and it would kill her. When she told him her plan, he had a "satisfied maniacal smile."

When she told her mom the next morning about Bob's wanting her to kill herself, her mom began to believe Kim. Her mom and Bob fought and he left for good. Kim's mom was able to get a day shift at the hospital and to be home nights. For the first time in a long time, Kim finally began to sleep at night. I saw a slight smile form on her face. I smiled back. Kim reported that being able to "get out" her story was helpful.

ADDRESS THE ABUSER

The next phase of therapy involved Kim addressing her abuser. I chose the Gestalt "empty chair" method. I asked Kim to imagine Bob sitting in a chair knowing that he could do no harm to her and she could say anything that came to her mind to him. I reassured her that this would help her feel stronger and lessen her anxiety and fear. I chose this method because, rather than "telling about" the experience, Kim could directly confront and speak to her abuser. This more direct approach is an empowering process that involves taking charge of the situation and standing up to the abuser.

Kim described Bob as slumped in the chair and expressionless. Then, she recounted in detail the horrible things Bob had done to her. She cried and expressed the emotions she had during the abuse and that she had carried inside since then. She described how the abuse had affected her emotionally, how she felt fearful and anxious, how it was hard for her to trust, how she was anxious with guys, how she felt about sex and how she even felt about physical touch and affection.

After this cathartic purging, Kim said, "I think I've told him all I want to tell him." Then I encouraged her to stand up and to declare that she was no longer his victim. Kim stood and strongly proclaimed several times, "You did horrible things to me, but you did not destroy me. What you did to me will not determine who I am. I am strong! I am strong!" She nodded at me with a determined expression.

I AM STRONG!

"He is gone. I don't see him. He is gone, and I am strong." She smiled with confidence. "I am strong!" became her motto. She said that she did indeed feel stronger. She stood up straighter and more confidently.

This beautiful, innocent-looking, intelligent, and courageous young woman had not only survived physical, emotional, mental, and sexual abuse, she was an amazingly strong person, and she was determined to have a fuller life that included relationships with guys. "Eventually, I'd like to marry and have children."

Kim's mother flew in from another state so the three of us could have a session. Her mother apologized for not believing her in the past and for not ever helping her to get professional therapy. Kim forgave her mother and reassured her that she was stronger than she'd ever been. Her mom smiled and said, "I believe you. I'm so proud of you." Kim also told her mother how much she appreciated all that she had done for her through the years. They hugged and expressed their love for each other.

ANXIETY WITH GUYS

Next, we addressed Kim's anxiety with guys. She learned to use breathing exercises to calm her anxious emotions and thoughts. After a few calming breaths, she inhaled "the spirit and strength of God" and exhaled "a calming sense of peace." This was her ritual several times each day, and when she felt anxious, her intentional breaths reminded her that she was in charge of her breathing and her life.

Kim planned how she would handle a date. One way was to tell the guy up front that she had been treated badly in the past and that she wanted him to be very respectful of her feelings and boundaries. "If he can handle that, I'll go out with him. If he can't, too bad for him."

An example of Kim's growing confidence was when she went to a formal dance with a date. "I let him put his hand around my waist as we danced, and I did hold his hand. He was very nice. I was a little nervous, but I felt strong and good. We had a really good time. We decided to go out again next week-end."

COURAGEOUS SPOKESPERSON

Kim did some powerful work during our time together. A true valedictory of her journey was her speech to university students about abuse. Without going into vivid detail, she told her story with courage, care, clarity, and words of encouragement for those who have been abused to get help.

WORDS TO LIVE BY

"Often, it isn't the initiating trauma that creates seemingly insurmountable pain, but the lack of support after." S. Kelley Harrell

"You can recognize survivors of abuse by their courage. When silence is so very inviting, they step forward and share their truth, so others know they are not alone." Jeanne McElvaney from "Healing Insights."

FOR PERSONAL REFLECTION:

- How can this story be helpful to you?
- What do you think is helpful in overcoming abuse?

For more questions see the Study Guide in the back of the book.

I've Got to Get Marriage Right This Time

We all carry with us painful experiences from our past that affect us personally, relationally, and professionally. The following story illustrates how desperation can lead a person to deal with his or her issues and ultimately have a fulfilling life.

WHAT'S WRONG WITH ME?

"This is my fourth marriage and I just turned forty. There must be something wrong with me. I've got to get it right this time"

Harold was a large, imposing, and successful attorney dressed in an expensive suit, but he had the deeply furrowed forehead of a troubled person. He quickly summarized each of his brief marriages. Then, he shrugged his shoulders, shook his head with disbelief, and asked, "Why does this keep happening to me?"

He said that he and his wife Darlene had been married for fourteen months. She was five years older than he, had been divorced for several years, and had two adopted teen-aged daughters. Harold wanted to prove to Darlene that he could get it right this time. While they dated, Harold was devoted to their relationship and his relationship with her daughters, but during their honeymoon in Tahiti, Harold started worrying about his law practice. He said Darlene told him she felt he was becoming "distant."

I'VE GOT TO FIGURE THIS OUT

Since returning from Tahiti, Harold had been working non-stop. Darlene told him that their marriage was not good, and that he must get help, or their marriage was finished. "I've got to figure this out," he said.

To help Harold "figure this out," I asked him about his childhood. He said that his dad died of a heart attack when he was eight. His father had owned a men's clothing store and worked such long hours that Harold barely knew him. Harold described his mother as "something else." She owned a successful business and financed Harold's education through private schools, college, and law school. "Mom smothered me, and she still wants to know everything I do. Darlene says my mother tries to control my life and that I let her."

WIFE'S PERSPECTIVE

Darlene came for her session. She was an attractive woman who presented a mature, reflective, and realistic description of their relationship. She explained that she waited a long time after her divorce to date and remarry. Harold's marital past made her skeptical about marrying him, but "he was so consistently dedicated to being responsible and good to me and to my daughters that I was convinced we could have a great marriage and family."

THINGS CHANGED

After they married, things changed. On their honeymoon, they were not intimate once and they still had not had sex. When she tried to address this issue with Harold, he said he was too tired. Darlene said that Harold was a workaholic. "That's all he thinks about...even at home." She described his mother as a control freak. "I feel like I have made such a big mistake and I am concerned how this is affecting my daughters. He has barely spent any time with them. He was so good to them when we dated, but he's in his own world of work and dutifully calling his mommy dearest."

SET AND ACHIEVE GOALS

At his next appointment, Harold said that he had been fortunate to be very successful in school and as an attorney with a great law practice, "but I am such a failure in marriage and with my family." A key to Harold's academic and professional success was his dedicated commitment to achievement. We first addressed how he could focus on "achievement" in his relationships.

We identified "undivided time with Darlene and the children" as crucial for their reconnection. Harold's goal was to have enough time for his work and to make the time to spend with his wife and the children. For Harold, this had to be specific, scheduled times...from 7:30 AM to 6 PM was work time, and from 6:30 PM to 10 PM was relationship time. To help him transition from work to home, Harold and Darlene took thirty-minute walks with their dogs. The combination of schedule and transition time helped him accomplish both work and family time.

DRIVEN WORKAHOLIC

When I asked Harold what "drove him" to be a workaholic, he said he did not know. With further exploration, Harold recalled that when his dad died, his mother told him, "Don't cry. You've got to focus on your schoolwork. Crying won't get you anywhere. You must work hard and make the best grades." Her deceased father had been a very successful attorney, and she wanted her son to have the "prestige and prominence" of being a very successful attorney. This command led Harold to the childhood decision: "Don't feel. Work hard." He lived this directive with only a few brief romantic exceptions.

UNRESOLVED GRIEF

The next step was to help Harold address his long-held grief over the loss of his father. When I asked him to tell me about memories of his dad, he said he had some Christmas memories. He told a story about being on the floor with his dad while they watched the electric train when he was six. He said, "My dad and I are watching the train go around the track and we are smiling at each other. I am so happy." Tears formed in Harold's eyes and he moaned a sad, "Oh. I missed my daddy so much." Harold unleashed a lifetime of stored tears. He cried for several minutes. He said, "I wished so much that I had had my daddy. Mom was so stern and controlling. All those times I wanted my daddy to be there."

After a long pause, Harold said, "Wow! There are a lot of feelings that I sealed off a long time ago. Sometimes on Father's Days I have felt twinges of emotion, but I've just shut them off and plowed into my work." This emotional release and the following grief work were turning points for Harold.

WRITE A LETTER

The second part of his grief work involved writing a letter to his dad. He wrote eight pages of detailed heartfelt feelings and memories to his dad. Then, he read them out loud as if his dad was sitting in a chair in my office. This emotional expression helped him voice his deeply held emotions. Then, I asked him what he thought his dad would say in response. Harold paused for a long time, looked at "his dad sitting in the chair" and said, "He'd hug me. He'd tell me that he loved me and was proud of my accomplishments. He'd tell me that he wished he'd spent more time with me. Then he'd smile at me and say that I've finally found a good woman and that I need to do what it takes to have a good marriage."

The session concluded when Harold smiled, "I feel like I've lost a fifty-pound weight I've been carrying inside. It was good to remember my daddy and to feel a loving connection with him…like he's really for me and he wants me to be a good husband and dad." This "loving connection" Harold felt with his dad helped to open the door for him to feel a "loving connection" with Darlene and her daughters.

SET BOUNDARIES

Harold had a hard time setting boundaries with his mother, so this was our next agenda. I brought to my office a washcloth, a hand towel, a bath towel, and a beach towel. Each of these towels represented boundaries. First, I asked large Harold to stand on a washcloth. This was a humorous balancing act for him, but it seriously represented the lack of boundary he had with his mother. She could push him around and he didn't have a leg to stand on. He commented, "This is what it's like with my mother. I just let her push me around and I'm always uncomfortable and I'm never able to stand my ground with her." I let him experience his uncomfortable and wobbly wash cloth boundary for a short while.

Next, I asked him to stand on a hand towel. This was a little more comfortable for him, but still there was no boundary without his mother being able to walk all over him. The bath towel gave Harold some breathing room. "I like this a lot better. I don't feel trapped. I can stand in a strong position. I can even move around on it, but my mother could still get too close." Finally, I laid the large beach towel on the floor. Harold smiled as he stepped onto it. "Now I can really feel better here. If I choose, I can let her come to the edge of the towel and I can choose to move to the other side away from her. Hey, it's large enough, if I want to, I can invite Darlene onto it with me when we want to be close to each other." This visual and "I can now stand my ground with my mother" feeling helped to equip Harold each time he encountered his mother.

ADULT RELATIONSHIP WITH HIS MOTHER

Harold's "mother work" also included a joint session with his mother where they concluded they needed to have an adult-to-adult relationship...finally. His mother only came to the one session, but she said, "I can now see that Harold is stronger emotionally. I know I can be a strong personality and a force to be reckoned with. Harold was my project and he's my only child. It's been hard to let go of him." She said she had expected Harold to be like an adult as a little child when her husband died. She dealt with her grief by working herself to death and she thought Harold should do the same. She apologized to Harold for her insensitive expectation. They shook hands; then hugged.

Standing straight and strong, Harold said, "Mom, I'll call you every week and we can invite you over to our house every few weeks. I love you. You've done so much for me, but it's time for us to have a healthier relationship that includes healthy boundaries. Dr. Parsons and I did this interesting exercise with towels." He described the exercise to his mother, and she said, "I think each of us will be better with our own beach towels." She smiled.

Their relationship included boundaries that they agreed would be healthier for them and for Harold's marriage. Harold later reported this emotionally freed him to feel a deeper and growing intimacy with his wife and a fatherly relationship with Darlene's daughters. Eventually, his mom and Darlene developed a workable relationship, not close, but a better relationship than it had been. They were both strong women, and they agreed to have respect for each other.

A LOVING AND INTIMATE MARRIAGE

Darlene loved and was committed to Harold, but she did not want a mother-son relationship with him. Therapy is usually about people making growth and changes in their lives and relationships. This was certainly the case for Harold and Darlene. Week after week they faithfully focused on these goals and they developed a marriage to last a lifetime. They even took a parenting class to help them with the challenges of rearing two teen-agers. I also had sessions with the girls and with them as a family and they "created" good relationships.

Together, Harold and Darlene developed a more equal relationship that included shared responsibilities, family time, and romantic and intimate dates. Their sex life became true lovemaking. A key to their intimacy was a touching exercise. They began by gently touching each other from the neck up and sharing loving and complimentary comments about each other's hair and face. Then they gave each other back rubs and massages followed by caressing arms and hands that added to their closeness. Next, they caressed and massaged each other's legs and feet. Before their next assignment, they reported, "We just couldn't wait any longer, so we had sex...the best lovemaking we've ever had." We laughed and high fived.

I FINALLY GOT IT RIGHT

They bought a small farm where they kept some animals and grew vegetables. This place became their getaway for fresh air and family fun. Harold learned to relax and truly enjoy life. An older man who owned an adjoining farm was the part-time caretaker of their animals, and he also became an enriching father figure for Harold. This wise old farmer taught Harold "the finer things of life:" how to and when to plant and care for their vegetable garden; how to care for their three heifers, two goats, and two llamas; and how to relax in a hammock. They also talked about the weather, the benefit for doing an honest day's work of physical labor, and the blessings of having a good woman and raising kids.

About a year after our concluding session, Harold wrote a note that said, "I finally got it right. This is what I always wanted."

WORDS TO LIVE BY

"In the grief that comes with recognizing what happened to us, we often feel there is nowhere to turn for solace...We do things to keep it away, such as becoming overly busy...to numb our feelings...We don't feel hope, but when we surrender to our sadness fully, hope trickles in." Maureen Brady, Beyond Survival

"I was cranked to a fifth gear, and everything I did, I did on a deadline." Mitch Albom, Tuesdays with Morrie

"We're not in this life just to work, we're in it to live." Cecelia Ahem, The Gift

FOR PERSONAL REFLECTION:

- How can this story be helpful to you?
- What do you think causes and helps workaholics?

For more questions see the Study Guide in the back of the book.

Putting the Family Back Together

When families are broken apart by divorce or other causes, each member is profoundly affected. The following story focuses on how a child helped put his family back together.

STARING INTO SPACE

Nine-year-old Cody's mom brought him to counseling because he often stared into space for long periods of time at home and at school. Carrie said that Cody had developed this behavior over the past year since she and Cody's dad divorced. At our initial session, Cody was engaging and inquisitive. When I asked him if he was aware that he "stared into space" for periods of time, he said he was only aware of it after his teacher or mom told him. "I don't know why I do it. I just do it, I guess."

THE MOVIE INSIDE

I asked him, if we had this super powerful, high-tech camera that could record what was going on in his mind during these times, what would we see. Cody "scanned" his mind for a couple of minutes. "We would see the movie about when my parents told us they were divorcing." I asked him to tell me about the "movie."

> "My mom and dad are in our family room and
> they tell my little brother and me they want to
> talk to us. I was eight and my little brother was
> six. My mom is crying, and my dad is nervous.
> They tell us they are going to divorce. My little
> brother runs screaming back to our bedroom and
> I run after him. I hold him and tell him that we
> will be okay. After that, my dad moves out the
> next day. Then, he comes back, and my mom and
> brother and I go to stay at my grandmother's
> house for a couple of weeks. Then we move into
> an apartment. That's what I think about
> sometimes. I guess I think about it a lot."

I told Cody that I really appreciated his sharing the story
and I asked him how he felt inside. I wondered how I could
be most helpful to Cody. He had told me that he liked to
make things with his hands, so I decided to give him some
clay at our next session to construct the traumatic scene.
This would allow him to tangibly create this scene that was
painfully stuck in his mind.

MAKE A MODEL OF THE SCENE

On a large sheet of cardboard on my office floor, Cody
constructed the scene with several boxes of clay. Over the
next two sessions, Cody carefully molded the sofa, chairs,
television set, and bedrooms, along with his mom, dad,
little brother, and himself.

I invited Cody's mother to come to our next session. She
was amazed at the exactness of his replica. Then, I asked
Cody to tell the story and to move the people as he told it.

"Here is Mom on the sofa crying and Dad is sitting next to her. Mom tells us that they are getting a divorce and that Dad is moving out. My little brother runs screaming to our bedroom (*he moved his brother figure to their bedroom*), and I follow him (*he moved his figure*), and I sit on the bed with him and tell him we will be okay. Mom comes in (*he moved his Mom figure*), and talks to us, and we hold my little brother. Then, Dad moves out (*he moved his dad figure to the far corner of the sheet*), and Mom and my brother, and I are in our house. Next, Dad moves back (*he moved his Dad figure into the house*). Then, Mom, and my brother, and I move to my grandparents' home and then into an apartment (*he moved the three figures to a far edge of the cardboard*). I feel really sad. I don't like it that my parents divorced."

THE FAMILY FELL APART

During all these moves, the clay figures of his mom, brother and dad began to fall apart, but his figure remained intact. I looked at his mom and she had tears in her eyes.

"This is what happened. I fell apart. His little brother fell apart. His dad fell apart. Our family fell apart. But Cody held it together and helped all of us. He's held all of this inside." She went over to Cody and held him. "I'm so sorry I have not been here for you. I've been such a mess. I've just tried to take care of myself and your brother.

I just thought you were so strong. You are strong, but you don't have to take care of us now. I'm here for you. I love you so much."

As Carrie held Cody, he began to cry. For the next several minutes, Cody released a bucket full of his feelings. They hugged, wiped each other's tears, blew their noses, and said loving words of support to each other. Carrie reassured Cody that she was doing okay and that every day he could tell her how he was feeling. Cody smiled and said, "I promise I will."

RECREATING THE FAMILY

At the next two sessions, Cody, his mom, and his brother sat on the floor and created with clay the new scene of their lives and their "together" selves. Each of their figures had smiles on their faces with their hands raised, "because we're happy," Cody said. They took their creation home and placed it on the coffee table in their family room as a positive reminder of their "new" lives. Cody no longer needed to stare into space.

We had several more family sessions. During these times, they planned ways to be open with each other, supportive of each other, loving to each other, and have lots of fun. They also decided to hold hands and have a family prayer each evening that would end with an "Amen hug." At our concluding session, Cody reported that his mom had bought him a case of clay, so he could continue his "clay creations." He presented me with one of them, "a super powerful, high-tech camera." We all laughed and hugged each other.

WORDS TO LIVE BY

"Families are about love overcoming emotional torture." Matt Groening, creator of *The Simpsons*

"Sometimes the best families are the ones God builds using unexpected pieces of our hearts." Melanie Shankle

FOR PERSONAL REFLECTION:

- How can this story be helpful to you?
- What do you think families can do to improve their lives and relationships?

For more questions see the Study Guide in the back of the book.

If you have ever lost a child, you know what most people say: "This is the greatest loss a person can experience." While I counseled with Conner, a surgeon, and Paige, a nurse, early in my practice, I will never forget this dear couple and the journey we shared.

SUDDEN INFANT DEATH

The couple's sunken, defeated, and emotionally drained facial expressions and body language said it all. Their two-month-old son had died from Sudden Infant Death Syndrome. Albert was their first born. Following a picture-perfect pregnancy, he was born healthy and robust. The painful shock of the sudden death of their completely loved precious creation was more than they could bear. Their grief was so devastating that they could barely utter words.

THEIR PAINFUL STORY

They began their story by saying what a wonderful evening they had had with Albert. Conner had held and rocked their son who carried the name of his hero, medical missionary and Nobel Peace Prize recipient, Dr. Albert Schweitzer. Paige added what a loving time she had breast feeding her baby whom she had carried inside her body for nine months. They described the details of burping him and changing his diaper, laying him in his crib, and watching him fall asleep. Conner said, "We just held each other that night as we admired this beautiful baby and said what a blessing God had given us."

Their tender smiles turned haunted. "We went to bed, and after an hour or so, I did not hear any breathing on the baby monitor. I sat up for a moment listening with my mommy ears and I heard nothing. I did not want to think there was a problem, but at the same time, I felt panicked. I shook Conner and told him we needed to check on Albert," Paige said.

Conner said, they quietly walked over to Albert's crib and he was "so still." He said he panicked, "Oh, my God! He's not breathing!" His medical mind kicked into alert and he immediately checked Albert for any life signs, and he started CPR. Paige called 911. "With all my years of training and saving people's lives, I tried and tried. I tried and tried to get him to breathe. Oh, God! I could not..."

WEEPING AND EMBRACING

Conner and Paige held onto each other as they wailed their deep grief. I moved from my chair and embraced them as we huddled and wept together. After several minutes, we wiped our eyes, blew our noses, and just breathed.

Paige related that she grew up singing in the children's choir at church. She said she believed in God and that if you did good things that nothing bad would ever happen. "I guess I was too naïve to think anything bad could ever happen to us. I just can't believe God wants this kind of devestation to happen."

Conner said that he may not have the kind of faith Paige has, "but we go to church and I pray. As a surgeon, I do what I can when I operate on people, and I leave the rest up to God."

I asked them how their faith helped them through this time. They said together, "We believe Albert is with God." Conner said, "I don't know exactly what that means, but I have to believe it." Paige added, "Heaven is only a concept for me, but I believe we really are spiritual beings with earthly bodies. This is what I believe, but I hurt like hell because I want my baby back. I just want him back." Conner and Paige sobbed and held each other.

Be Present

I told them I could only imagine how horrible this was for them and that I appreciated all they had shared with me. I added that I did not have any easy answers for them, but that I would be with them in their grief. They nodded with knowing expressions. This was the sad beginning of sharing with this dear couple who were devastated. I simply journeyed with them through the process as they grieved and grew.

> *We discussed that you really don't get over grief, but you do what you can to get through it.*

Mourning Partners

During my first couple of sessions with Paige and Conner, I shared with them a term I had learned while working as a chaplain at Parkland Hospital: "mourning partner." The term was offered to them as a couple as they mourned as partners in their grief. The term is also fitting for the friend, care giver, or professional. It fit for the three of us in this situation.

To be a mourning partner simply means being present with the grieving persons, sitting with them, touching their hands as is appropriate, and listening to them. You may also tear up with them and care for them in their grief. This is usually accompanied by a box of tissues. Not many words can help in the early stages of such a horrible loss. I encouraged them to share their feelings and their memories.

STAGES OF GRIEF

Eventually, we discussed "the stages of grief" developed by Dr. Elisabeth Kubler-Ross, the author of *On Death and Dying.* While I was a chaplain at Parkland Hospital, I met with Dr. Kubler-Ross during her visit to Dallas. Although Paige and Conner were medical professionals familiar with the stages of grief, they sometimes asked if what they were experiencing was "normal." I shared this process with them in their deep personal grief to help them identify the "normalcy" of their feelings.

SHOCK

We started with the initial stage of shock. Because of the suddenness of Albert's death, Conner and Paige's state of shock and disbelief lasted quite a while. "We feel like we're in a daze and just going through the motions of daily life." They wished they would wake up and know it was a bad dream. "No wonder," I told them.

IF ONLY

Bargaining and the "if only" stage really gripped these medically trained professionals. They shared how they had years of training and experience to help save lives, but they could not save their own son. They felt so helpless and wondered, "If only we had checked on him earlier. If only we had him in bed with us, maybe we would have detected this in time."

DEPRESSION

Depression and emptiness lasted longer for both Paige and Conner. They shared the deep sadness they felt that was so heavy and empty at the same time. I encouraged them to feel as sad as they needed and to let their tears flow. "Albert has only been outside of my body for such a short while that I either expect him to be inside of me or in his crib. Many times I just sit in the rocking chair and hold a pillow," Paige said. Conner added, "Many times we just sit and cry." Sometimes they "took turns," with one expressing the sad feelings while the other gave comfort. Other times they "felt miserable together."

ANGER

They experienced varying degrees of anger which was a primary part of Conner's grief. I encouraged him to "let out" his anger at God, at himself, and at the unfairness of an innocent child having to die. He verbally expressed these bitter feelings in my office, in his car, and whenever else he needed. Paige wrote her angry feelings in a journal that helped her release them "sentence by sentence."

ACCEPTANCE

Acceptance does not mean a person is "ok" about the loss of a loved one, it just means accepting the reality of the situation. Conner and Paige said their medical experience both helped and made it harder for them to accept Albert's death. "We discuss some of the patients we've lost. We have seen a number of people die, and those who loved them just can't bring them back. Now we know this in a very personal way. It never gets easy."

HOPE: WHAT THEY COULD DO

While Paige and Conner grieved their great loss, they looked at what they could do to move on with their lives. They cried whenever the tears came. They tried to eat healthily, took walks, looked at pictures of Albert, and even put together an album with these photos. "Looking at all these pictures helps us and makes us sad at the same time," Paige said.

They discussed how their family and friends from their church and hospital were supportive. They shared their faith struggles and strengths. They found ways of honoring Albert through a charity and a research project for SIDS. About a year later, they made plans to have other children.

GREATEST LOSS

The loss of a child may be the greatest loss of all. Through the years I have counseled many parents who have lost children from miscarriages, infant deaths, and deaths at every age of childhood, adolescence, young adulthood, middle age, and older. They have died from being too young and fragile, SIDS, congenital conditions, brain tumors, and other cancers. Some have died from heart attacks, strokes, seizures, climatic exposure, drowning, and various kinds of accidents. Others have been lost due to drug overdoses, suicides, murders, wars, and unknown causes and natural causes. They are all hard!

THE REST OF THE STORY

Conner and Paige held precious memories of Albert and missed him so much. They experienced the worst heartache they could imagine...the death of their child. Years later they said, "We still miss Albert, and we have made it through this great loss as best we can." Eventually they had two other children and they shared the pictures and stories of Albert with them.

WORDS TO LIVE BY

"Only people who are capable of loving strongly can also suffer great sorrow, but this same necessity of loving serves to counteract their grief and heals them." Leo Tolstoy

How very softly you tiptoed into our world, almost silently, only a moment you stayed. But what an imprint your footsteps have left upon our hearts." Dorothy Ferguson

FOR PERSONAL REFLECTION:

- How can this story be helpful to you?
- What do you think about the greatest losses?

For more questions see the Study Guide in the back of the book.

The Struggling Recovering Alcoholic

What are your thoughts about or experiences with alcohol, alcoholism, and addictions? These three "A's" affect all of us directly or indirectly. The following is one person's story that portrays the struggle and hope of dealing with alcohol.

JIM'S STORY

Jim had been out of rehab for one month and was struggling. He said that he owned his own business and for years had bought whiskey on his way to his office. He explained that for the past ten to twelve years he would start drinking about 4 o'clock every afternoon and miraculously was able to drive home. Eventually, he would pass out. He went to rehab for a month and said that he wanted to stay sober. "Every day is a battle. I'm going to AA five or six times a week and that helps, but I need more help. My sponsor told me to come see you. I'm a forty-four-year-old arrogant, insecure, know-it-all, scared to death guy...I'm an alcoholic."

When I asked Jim what he did in rehab, he said he did Twelve Step work, met with a counselor and read the Big Book every day. Although he was a college graduate, he said he hated reading books. "I have to read damn reports all day long, so the last thing I want to do is read a book." I asked if he prayed while he was in rehab. He chuckled, "I prayed a lot while I was in there...to get out."

Jim's father was an alcoholic and his parents divorced when he was eleven. "Mom got tired of putting up with him. I don't want to wind up like my dad who died at forty-seven from cirrhosis of the liver. He drank himself to death." Although Jim had had a few long-term relationships that he described as "usually stormy," he had never married. Jim shared that he did not have a religious affiliation, "but I really need God's help to do what I don't seem to be able to do myself."

GET ON MY KNEES

Knowing that praying is usually a part of recovery programs, I asked if it would help him to pray. He said he thought it would. He smiled, "I guess it helped me get out of rehab, but I just don't remember to pray. Being the arrogant S.O.B. that I am, I probably need to get on my knees if I'm going to pray." Jim said he was desperate because it took everything in his power to turn his car in the direction to go to his office every morning rather than turning in the direction of the liquor store.

We brainstormed about what he could do so he would remember to pray every morning. Finally, we came up with the idea that every night before he went to bed, he would put his car keys under the bed. The next morning, he would have to "get on his knees to retrieve his keys." While he was on his knees he would remember to pray. This worked! Every morning his prayer was, "God, help me turn my car in the right direction. Amen."

After a few weeks, Jim came to a session beaming, "Doc, I'm doing better at this praying thing than we even thought. Hell, I get on my knees every night to put my keys under my bed. So, I thought, while I'm on my knees by my bed at night, I had just as well pray then, too. Now, I'm praying every morning and every night for God to help me turn my car in the right direction. I also pray this prayer on my way to my office. This is working. I plan to keep it up." Praying, counseling, and AA helped Jim keep turning in the right direction.

DON'T FEEL

While Jim was making significant progress, underneath he still carried a lot of emotional pain. When I asked him how he felt as a little kid, he explained that he tried not have any feelings. He recalled being scared and sad and crawling under the covers in his bed while his parents were having drunken fights. "That's what I did then and that's what I've been doing all my life. To avoid feeling scared, I try not to feel at all, and I escape into sleep or passing out."

Week by week Jim addressed the pain and emptiness he had carried since childhood, and he chose a feeling each week that he could feel and fill up the hole inside. Eventually, Jim said, "Feelings in moderation can be my friend." As he shared his feelings with his girlfriend, their relationship improved. She attended Al Anon meetings and they developed a common language and a deeper understanding of themselves and each other.

ONE DAY AT A TIME

Jim kept in touch with me for some time after we

concluded our official counseling sessions. He brought me one of his company calendars each Christmas with a little note saying, "I still get on my knees every night and every morning...one day at a time I'm still sober." Beside his signature he'd drawn a little key. The last I heard, Jim and his girlfriend were together, and Jim was still sober and an AA sponsor. I've shared Jim's "get on my knees to retrieve my keys" story with a lot of addicts. Thanks, Jim.

WORDS TO LIVE BY

"If your knees knock, kneel." AA

"It works if you work it, so work it because you're worth it." AA

"Above all the grace and gifts that Christ gives to his beloved is that of overcoming self." Saint Francis of Assisi

---

FOR PERSONAL REFLECTION:

- How can this story be helpful to you?
- What do you think about addictions?

For more questions see the Study Guide in the back of the book.

Coming Out

While there are various viewpoints about what causes a person to be gay, or what causes sexual orientation in general, Warren's story is similar to that of many people I have counseled over the years. His story contains some of the issues, struggles, and courage of a remarkable person who is gay.

WILL YOU JUDGE ME?

Warren sat anxiously in a waiting room chair. When he sat in my office during our session, he continued to appear unusually nervous. This nice looking, somewhat overweight thirty-five-year-old man shared that he had suffered from depression since childhood but had mostly functioned successfully in school, college, and in his computer programming work.

During this initial session, we explored Warren's depressive symptoms and history and his conflicted relationship with his father. At the conclusion of our meeting, Warren said, "My pastor who referred me to you told me that you are not judgmental and that you could handle whatever issue I have." I told Warren that I would not judge him, that I was glad he had come to therapy, and that I could handle what he needed to address. I sensed that Warren had sexual orientation concerns.

SAFE PLACE

About mid-way through out next session, Warren said, "I have never told anyone this before and I have been in agony for years. I want to believe that you will not judge me for what I need to tell you." I commended Warren for his courage, reassured him that this was a safe place, and said that I was here to help him.

"I'm gay," he wailed from the depth of his being. After a few minutes of my gentle and caring words, Warren looked at me with red childlike eyes and said, "You don't think I'm a bad person...that I'm going to hell, do you? I go to church. I pray these pleading prayers." I told Warren that I did not think he was a bad person, that I could only imagine the agony he had gone through for years, and that I would help him. "Thank you," he whispered.

I THINK I WAS BORN THIS WAY

Warren's spoken secret opened the door for his therapeutic journey. He shared how he had always felt "different."

> "Boys made fun of me and called me a sissy, but I can remember feeling so attracted to a cute little boy in my second-grade class...I just wanted to hug him. It really wasn't sexual. I was so young, but I just loved him and thought about

him...like having a crush. I think I was depressed then. My mom took me to a child psychiatrist because I was 'withdrawn and had sleep problems.' I don't really remember much about those times. Do you think I'm horrible...that I was even horrible then?"

I reassured him that I did not think he was horrible. "Good," he said. "I think I was born this way. I guess God made me this way. I don't understand."

PAINFUL ADOLESCENCE

By adolescence, Warren reported that he had very strong sexual attraction to other boys and to one of his male teachers, "but I never did anything or said anything to anybody. At night I wondered why I felt these feelings and I felt I must be a bad person...that something horrible was wrong with me."

Through his years with his family, Warren's father cursed about "fags," and he and Warren's brother made fun of homosexuals. "I just pulled into my shell and never said anything about homosexuality."

CONDEMNATION FROM THE CHURCH

Another issue Warren had: "A lot of Christian folks condemn homosexuals." He said that he and his family had attended a church until he was in the seventh grade where the minister preached about "the evils of homosexuality...they are of the devil and the fires of hell await them unless they change their sinful ways." Those words were seared into Warren's mind.

What Did Jesus Say?

I asked Warren if he had a "red letter" edition of the Bible where the words of Jesus in the Gospels are printed in red. He said that he did. His homework was to find what Jesus said about homosexuality.

When he returned for the next session with his Bible, he reported that he could not find anything that Jesus said about homosexuality. We smiled, and Warren said, "Well, that helps a lot. Maybe Jesus would not condemn me. Maybe Jesus would even love me." While media reports and various church pronouncements about the "evils" of homosexuality affect Warren, he knows he was "born this way. I did not choose to be gay. In fact, I have tried and prayed not to be gay, but it is how I am. I still get depressed about it, but I no longer think I'm evil or going to hell."

Warren is now active in a church that operates from a "don't ask, don't tell" position. He and his pastor have a trusting and close relationship. He says, "I now believe in a God of love and grace. I love singing hymns. I like going to church. This church is so much more open-minded than the church we attended when I was a boy. Thank God!"

Telling Family

"Coming out" to his parents was one of Warren's biggest hurdles. His mother lovingly responded by saying, "Honey, I think I've known this for a long time, but I did not want to say anything. I'm just so sorry for you that you won't be able to have the kind of life you wanted. I love you...I always have, and I always will." Warren was thankful and relieved that his mother responded the way she did. Unbeknownst to Warren, his mother told his dad that Warren was going to talk with him about an important issue and that he had better not be an "ass" when they talked.

This warning from his mother to his dad probably prevented Warren's "coming out" from being the blood bath he had feared. Warren said that his Dad was still a "jerk" when he told him, "but at least he wasn't the ranting, raving, cursing, and judgmental bigot the he could have been." His dad did not say that he loved or accepted Warren, "but at least it wasn't his usual reign of terror."

After a few months, Warren's dad told him that he did love him. Warren reported that his dad said, "Son, I still don't understand this homosexual stuff, but you are my son and I love you." They even hugged. Warren said that his brother and his family are members of a church that "condemns homosexuality." He talked with his brother and sister-in-law about how he had prayed for years not to be gay. "I think they are coming to see that I am not a bad person because I'm gay. And they know I'm a great uncle to their daughter."

ADDRESSING DEPRESSION

Depression has a long history in Warren's family. His mother, his aunt, and his grandmother have had serious, and almost chronic episodes of depression. Warren's therapy process and anti-depressant medications have helped his level of depression to lessen and to stabilize to a great degree. While his work history has had its ups and downs, Warren steadily focuses on keeping a job or finding a new one when a contract ends.

Underlying much of Warren's difficulties has been his sense of worth. "I don't think I've ever felt good enough in Dad's eyes or in my own. I have always felt different and that something was wrong with me. For so many years, I thought God looked at me the same way my dad did...and then there is the whole issue with homosexuality." Step by step, Warren progressed toward believing that he is a worthwhile human being. He continues to courageously address his issues and to believe that he is a beloved child of God.

We still meet monthly, and Warren works very hard to stay on track and to keep growing to be the best person he can be. When he sits in my waiting room, Warren does not look anxious and depressed. He says with confidence, "This is my safe place and I'm glad to be here. Now what I need to address today is..."

ACCEPTANCE, HOPE, JOY

Warren's depression, dad issues, and damnation themes shifted more and more to increasing themes of acceptance, hope, and joy. Warren especially enjoys Christmas...a time to celebrate birth and to decorate his apartment with his many Christmas decorations. In fact, he keeps some of them on display throughout the year to remind him of "good things." Warren has come a long way. His words are, "I'm coming out more and more to be a whole and healthy person."

WORDS TO LIVE BY

"The closet does have a benefit. It provides safety. Which at times is important. But remember, as long as you are in there, two other things will be too, Fear and Shame." Anthony Ven-Brown from *A Life of Unlearning-a Preacher's Struggle with His Homosexuality, Church, and Faith*.

For I am convinced that...not anything in all creation will be able to separate us from the love of God..." Romans 8:38-39

FOR PERSONAL REFLECTION:

- How can this story be helpful to you?
- What are your thoughts about sexual orientation?

For more questions see the Study Guide in the back of the book..

The Bi-Polar Clown

If you have ever had depressive thoughts or feelings, you know what it's like. It is very common. Of course, varying degrees of depression and types of depression can include mood swings. It is important for all of us to have a compassionate and informed understanding of these conditions. The following story may tug at your heart and make you smile.

JILL'S DEPRESSION

"I'm a bi-polar clown." I've counseled many depressed and bi-polar people over the years, but I'd not heard that combination of terms. When Jill noted my puzzled expression, she explained in her soft and slow manner that she had been diagnosed with depression many years ago and as bi-polar a few years ago. She tended to be a lot more depressed than manic. She said that she had done volunteer clown ministry for over ten years. "My character is 'Happy Clown.' I used to clown at Vacation Bible Schools, for Sunday school classes, for children's programs, and for birthday parties. I haven't done that the past couple of years because I've been so depressed. I barely make it financially with two part-time jobs. I've not taken medication in quite a while. I guess I just need some help."

Jill faithfully attended her weekly counseling appointments as she traveled by a public transportation bus. We found a psychiatrist who agreed to prescribe her medication, and the service agency that referred her agreed to pay for her prescriptions. While Jill was never seriously suicidal during our year together, she struggled to keep her mood up and remain productive at her jobs. On a depression mood scale in which "10" is good and "0" means death or suicide, Jill's mood ranged from a 2 to a 7.

PAINFUL FAMILY SITUATION

Jill had divorced from an abusive husband when she was thirty. Her only child from that marriage was now in his mid-twenties and lived in the Pacific Northwest near his father's wealthy family. Jill grieved that she did not have a relationship with her son. "Although I know his dad was abusive to me, I was depressed during those years and I know I was not the kind of mother I wanted to be." Jill faithfully wrote to her son, but he never responded. "At least I'm doing now what I can do to let him know I love him and care about him. It's painful, but it helps me to just send those little notes to him."

FIND A CHURCH

As we explored ways for Jill to improve her life, she shared that she loved children and had enjoyed going to church. She agreed to find a church close to her government subsidized apartment. Two weeks later, Jill proudly declared that she had found a small neighborhood church. "They have good music. The people were friendly.

The preacher preached a good sermon. I think they have a good children's program. Maybe I could work in their nursery or even do some clown ministry."

I'm Not Cut Out for Church

When Jill came to her next session, I could tell that she was really depressed. She took her seat and stared at the floor with a sad and flat facial expression. Jill looked up at me with tears in her eyes and said, "It's just not going to work out. I thought I could do something good, but I just can't. I love the Lord, but maybe I'm just not cut out for the church."

She paused for a few moments and explained that after the church service, she told the preacher that she was glad to finally be back in church, and that she would be glad to help in their nursery. "I guess I was stupid because I also told him that I had depression, was on medication, was seeing a counselor, and doing better than I had in a long time. I said that I loved children a lot and that I had done clown ministry. I guess I said too much." The minister told her that depression was of the devil and that she had to get her soul right with Jesus before she could ever work with children. "It just knocked me down. I love the Lord, but I cannot go back to that church. Am I a bad person?" Jill stared at me with childlike disbelief. Her mood dropped from a six plus to "barely a two."

Reassurance and Faith

I felt sad for Jill and mad at the preacher. After reassuring Jill that she was not a bad person, I asked her why she thought the pastor had those ideas. "Maybe he just doesn't understand about depression. Maybe he believes what he told me, but I don't think the Bible says that depression is evil." I affirmed her faith and said, "So your faith is in the Lord. Is that right?" Jill said, "Oh, yes." I clarified, "So, your faith is not in that minister who does not understand depression. Is that right?" A little smile crept across her face and with a twinkle in her eyes, she said, "Yes."

I'll Go Back to That Church

After discussing the matter for several minutes, Jill said with a humble, but determined voice, "Maybe I'll go back to that church. It is God's house; not that pastor's church. God knows my depression is not of the devil. I believe God will give me the strength." While Jill worked on her issues, week after week, she continued to go to church. She enjoyed the music and the warmth and friendliness of the people...and some of the sermons. One day, she reported that the minister had not been at the church for four weeks in a row. The assistant minister announced that the pastor was ill. Jill said that she had been praying for the pastor.

Amazing Experience

At the next session, Jill shared a very unusual story. She said that the pastor was back in the pulpit and "just poured out his heart." He said that he had been so depressed that he had not been able to preach. His wife stood with him and she shared that she had been having an affair and that her husband had found out. She said that she and her husband were going to counseling to heal their marriage. Then the pastor confessed that he had been so wrong and judgmental about people who have depression or mental illness. He said that he had learned a lot from his counselor about depression and that he wanted to apologize to the congregation and "to one special and unnamed person" for his judgmental words. One of the deacons joined them at the pulpit and said that the church was going to support the pastor and his wife and love them as they walked through their dark valley. Jill could hardly believe her ears. After church, the pastor apologized to her. "We cried and hugged. Isn't that something!?"

A few weeks after that amazing experience, Jill and the pastor met and talked. He told Jill that he thought his mother had been depressed, but he did not understand it then. The pastor confided to Jill that he and his wife were making progress in their marriage counseling and he was less depressed. He also said that he would be glad for Jill to work in the church nursery and that he wanted to learn more about clown ministry. "Maybe the Lord used little old me to help him in some way."

CANCER

Jill's mood became mostly stable and she started a clown ministry at the church, but a few months later, she became physically ill. After several medical tests, it was determined that she had pancreatic cancer. I helped her write a letter to her older brother in Minnesota who offered for her to come and live with him and his wife. They agreed they would help her with medical treatment. Jill wept with gratitude.

The week before her move, Jill and I talked with her brother on the phone. He said, "Jill was the youngest and the forgotten child in the family. As her older brother, the least I can do now is to help her."

While in Minnesota, Jill and I kept in telephone contact during the last months of her life. We recounted the times we had shared, and she laughed when we talked about "Happy Clown." Our last visit was the day before she died. It was a soft, tender, and loving conversation with Jill saying that she was ready to "pass on to heaven." I cried and smiled at the same time.

AN INSPIRATION

At our final session before she left for Minnesota, Jill gave me a small needlepoint design she had crafted. I keep it on a shelf in my office. Jill was one of the sweetest people I have ever known. While she lived with sadness, economic challenges, mental illness, depression, and, eventually, a terminal illness, Jill had courage, a deep faith, and a shy child-like smile that brought joy to me and to a lot of other people. I'll never forget her introduction, "I'm a bi-polar clown." What an inspiration!

WORDS TO LIVE BY

"The clowns remind us with a tear and a smile that we share the same human weakness. Those peripheral people who by their humble saintly lives evoke a smile and awaken hope." Henri Nouwen from Clowning in Rome.

Mental illness is not a choice, but recovery is. National Alliance on Mental Illness (NAMI)

FOR PERSONAL REFLECTION:

- How can this story be helpful to you?
- What do you think will help people better understand mental illness?

For more questions see the Study Guide in the back of the book.

PART TWO

STUDY GUIDE

INTRODUCTION

The purpose of this section of the book is to offer you the opportunity to delve deeper into the stories and the issues that are addressed in each chapter. The questions are designed for your personal, professional, or group work. The *Words to Live By* are quotes to stimulate your thoughts and discussion, and the *For Further Reflection* offers additional resources on the topic. I hope the combination of the stories in this book, the tools in this section, and your own life experiences will enrich you in helpful and even life-changing ways.

This book is intended to be helpful in the scope of its purpose to inform and guide the reader, but it is not designed as a substitute for professional diagnosis or treatment. If you or someone you encounter exhibits troubling behaviors similar to those related in some of these stories, please obtain treatment from a trained professional.

Meet People Where They Are!

CONNECTING WITH THE BOOK

❖ How can this story be helpful to you?

❖ Do you identify with anyone in the story?

❖ What do you think about meeting people where they are?

CONNECTING WITH DAILY LIFE

❖ Have you or someone you know been hurt by a church or people in the community?

❖ What do you think about holding grudges?

❖ How can you let people know you care about them?

❖ What are some good questions to ask so you can get to know a person better?

❖ Why do you think we avoid or are afraid of meeting people where they are?

❖ Do you wish you had known better in the past about doing or not doing something?

❖ How do you need to have more courage?

❖ How can you be more compassionate?

WORDS TO LIVE BY

❖ Respond to paraphrase of Leo Tolstoy:

> *The most necessary person is the one with whom you are, and the most important act is to do good to another person, because for that purpose alone we were sent into this life!*

FOR FURTHER REFLECTION

Unafraid, by Adam Hamilton

Take Care of Yourself!

CONNECTING WITH THE BOOK
- ❖ How can this story be helpful to you?
- ❖ How is your self-care?

CONNECTING WITH DAILY LIFE
- ❖ How well do you take good care of yourself: (Scale 0-10)
  __Physically __Mentally __Emotionally __Relationally
  __Professionally or Vocationally __Spiritually
- ❖ Which areas will you strive to improve and how?

Now make notes and commitments to take good care in each of these areas.
- ❖ What is your life-giving sanctuary?
- ❖ Do you have hobbies or interests that give you a break?
- ❖ What helps you stay sane?
- ❖ How do or did you deal with traumatic situations?
- ❖ What helps or would help you cope with personal and/or professional stress?
- ❖ Do you take necessary safety precautions?
- ❖ What gives you joy, fulfillment, and meaning?
- ❖ Do you keep thank you notes and words of affirmation?

WORDS TO LIVE BY
- ❖ Respond to the logic of why we should take care of ourselves for the sake of the other:
  *When you do, you'll have the energy to spare to do
  a lot of good with love and care.* [1]

FOR FURTHER REFLECTION
Younger Next Year by Chris Crowley and Henry S. Lodge

Shut Up and Listen!

CONNECTING WITH THE BOOK

❖ How can this story be helpful to you?

❖ How well do you listen? If you're not sure, check it out.

❖ What will you do to be a better listener?

CONNECTING WITH DAILY LIFE

❖ What do you think about listening being an art and a skill that requires practice?

❖ What do you think about a good listener giving undivided attention?

❖ What do you think about listening with patience and consideration?

❖ Why do you think it is so hard to listen well?

❖ What do you think about waiting to respond until the other person has finished speaking?

❖ What do you think about paying attention to the content and the feelings that are being expressed?

❖ What do you think about the blessings of listening?

WORDS TO LIVE BY

❖ Respond to the statement by Paul Tillich:
   "The first duty of love is to listen."

FOR FURTHER REFLECTION

W.A.I.T—Why Am I Talking? A Ted TALK

If They Stay Married, It Will Be A Miracle!

CONNECTING WITH THE BOOK

❖ How can this story be helpful to you?

❖ What do you think about the referring minister's comments about the couple's marriage possibilities?

❖ How do you think imagining the other person as a little child can help with understanding and compassion?

CONNECTING WITH DAILY LIFE

❖ What do you think about moving from survival instincts to becoming relational?

❖ What do you think are key internal factors that can help people make significant changes in their lives and relationships?

❖ How do you think AA, NA, SLAA, and similar programs can be helpful?

❖ What do you think about couples making daily commitments to their marriage?

❖ What do you think about "names of endearment?"

❖ What do you think are benefits of couples praying with/for each other?

WORDS TO LIVE BY

❖ Respond to the statement by Barbara De Angelis:
   "Marriage is not a noun; it's a verb. It isn't something you get. It's something you do. It's the way you love your partner every day."

FOR FURTHER REFLECTION

The Intimacy Jungle: How You Can Survive and Thrive in a Lasting Marriage by Terry Parsons

I May Have Caused My Dad's Death!

CONNECTING WITH THE BOOK

❖ How can this story be helpful to you?

❖ What are your thoughts about guilt?

❖ What do you think about guilt compounding the effects of grief?

CONNECTING WITH DAILY LIFE

❖ How do you think guilt can be helpful or harmful?

❖ What do you think about "overactive guilt glands?"

❖ How can talking about a loved one who has died be helpful?

❖ What do you think about the "empty chair" exercise of talking to the person who has died?

❖ What do you think can be helpful in dealing with guilt?

WORDS TO LIVE BY

❖ Respond to the statement by Mark Twain:
> *"Forgiveness is the fragrance that the violet sheds on the heel that has crushed it."*

FOR FURTHER REFLECTION

Forgiveness: Finding Peace through Letting Go by Adam Hamilton

The Vivid Dream!

CONNECTING WITH THE BOOK

❖ How can this story be helpful to you?

❖ What do you think about Lindsay's dream?

CONNECTING WITH DAILY LIFE

❖ What do you think about dreams?

❖ What do you think about troubling or recurring dreams?

❖ How do you think exploring dreams can provide insight or meaning?

❖ What do you think about replacement dreams?

❖ What do you think about the items in "A Basic Tool to Explore Your Dreams?"

❖ What do you think your dreams are telling you?

WORDS TO LIVE BY

❖ Respond to these statements about dreams:

"The dream is a little hidden door in the innermost and most secret recesses of the soul." Carl Jung

Dreaming is physiological but the content of the dreams is psychological and is a product of the dreamer's unconscious mind in collaboration with conscious experience.

FOR FURTHER REFLECTION

God, Dreams, and Revelation by Morton Kelsey

Memories, Dreams, Reflections by Carl Jung

The Scientific Study of Dreams: Neural Networks, Cognitive Development and Content Analysis by G. William Domhoff

Silence!

CONNECTING WITH THE BOOK

❖ How can this story be helpful to you?

❖ What do you think about silence in the conversation with Janie?

❖ When have you felt uncomfortable with silence?

CONNECTING WITH DAILY LIFE

❖ What contributes to your being comfortable or uncomfortable with silence?

❖ How can silence be both uncomfortable and golden?

❖ How can silence be helpful in personal or professional dialogue?

❖ How can personal times of silence benefit you?

❖ What do you think about silence as a form of meditation or prayer?

❖ What do you think about the still small voice inside?

❖ What do you think about the blessings of silence?

WORDS TO LIVE BY

❖ Respond to the statement by Janie:

"While I was lying here (in silence), that thought (of dancing) came into my mind."

FOR FURTHER REFLECTION

The Sound of Silence, Music and lyrics by Paul Simon

Up from the Bathroom Floor!

CONNECTING WITH THE BOOK

❖ How can this story be helpful to you?

❖ What do you think it takes to become empowered?

CONNECTING WITH DAILY LIFE

❖ What are your thoughts about abusive marriages and relationships?

❖ What are important tools, boundaries, and resources if one is in an abusive relationship?

❖ What do you think about the therapist's insights, reactions, role, and work?

❖ What are creative and practical ways to be more empowered?

❖ What do you think about Donald Duck and Wonder Woman?

❖ What do you think about this couple divorcing?

❖ How do you want to become more empowered?

WORDS TO LIVE BY

❖ Respond to this statement by Jan:

"I've been crowned by God and nobody is stronger than God."

FOR FURTHER REFLECTION

The Emotionally Abusive Relationship by Beverly Engel

Suicide Prevention!

CONNECTING WITH THE BOOK
- ❖ How can this story be helpful to you?
- ❖ What has helped you to not harm or kill yourself?

CONNECTING WITH DAILY LIFE
- ❖ Be aware of direct or veiled threats, previous attempts, giving away possessions, stockpiling means for suicide, self-mutilation, drug and alcohol abuse.
- ❖ Be aware of severe depression, significant losses, desperation about relationship issues and family situations
- ❖ Ways to help: Be willing to listen. Be non-judgmental. Allow them to express their feelings. Affirm their value or worth. Don't' be afraid to ask how depressed they are or if they have had thoughts about or had a plan for self-harm or suicide. Ask what has helped or will help them to not commit suicide. Get help from professionals or agencies skilled in suicide prevention. Call 911 when necessary.
- ❖ If you are ever suicidal, get help ASAP.

WORDS TO LIVE BY
- ❖ Respond to this statement:
    "When you feel like giving up, just remember the reason why you held on for so long."

FOR FURTHER REFLECTION
Volumes of information about suicide prevention can be found online, at suicide prevention hotlines, from qualified professionals, PsychAlive resource, and books like *Managing Suicidal Risk* by David A. Jobes

I'd Rather Kick!

Connecting with the Book

❖ How can this story be helpful to you?

❖ How do you deal with stored feelings?

Connecting with Daily Life

❖ How do you think troubled marriages or divorcing parents affect children?

❖ What do you think about feeling pulled apart by parents?

❖ What do you think about the myriad feelings James held inside?

❖ What do you think about his need to feel that he and his words were valued?

❖ What do you think helps a child feel secure and valued?

❖ What do you think about "blasting" his trumpet teacher?

❖ What do you think about kicking cardboard boxes and other means of releasing feelings?

❖ What do you think about the importance of an amicable divorce?

Words to Live By

❖ Respond to this statement by Cathy Meyer:

"In dealing with a child who is angry about your divorce: Love your child and be there for them even if their words are hurtful...your child's feelings, regardless of how negative, are more important than your feelings."

For Further Reflection

The Mad Family Gets Their Mad Out by Lynne Namka, Ed. D

Survivors of Suicide!

CONNECTING WITH THE BOOK

❖ How can this story be helpful to you?
❖ What do you think is helpful for survivors of suicide?

CONNECTING WITH DAILY LIFE

❖ Have you ever had someone close to you commit suicide?
❖ How did/does the suicide affect you?
❖ How do you think grief is compounded by suicide?
❖ What do you think about each person in the family?
❖ What do you think about what was helpful for each of them?
❖ What do you think about their progression of emotions through the grief process?
❖ What do you think about helpful expressions, activities, rituals, and family bonding?
❖ What do you think about loving one's self and each other?
❖ What do you think about their commitment to mental health?

WORDS TO LIVE BY

❖ Respond to these statements:

"You get through it. Day by day. Sometimes moment by moment."

"One day...You'll be able to remember the good things about your loved one and not just the end."

FOR FURTHER REFLECTION

Survivors of Suicide Support Groups (SOS)
American Association of Suicidology Books and Resources for Survivors

We Go for the Jugular!

1.

CONNECTING WITH THE BOOK

❖ How can this story be helpful to you?

❖ How do you deal with conflict?

CONNECTING WITH DAILY LIFE

❖ How did you family deal with conflict when you were growing up?

❖ What are triggers for your anger or other strong emotions?

❖ How do you see unresolved issues from the past sabotaging relationships?

❖ What do you think about "going for the jugular?"

❖ Why do you think some couples fight so horribly and destructively?

❖ What do you think motivates people to change?

❖ What do you think about the importance of 1) empathy, 2) apology, 3) forgiveness, 4) daily commitment?

❖ What do you think about this couple's swearing on the Bible their sacred vows to each other?

❖ What do you think about their kissing each other's neck every day?

❖ What do you think are healthy ways to deal with conflict?

WORDS TO LIVE BY

❖ Respond to this statement from James 1:9:
    "You must all be quick to listen, slow to speak, and slow to get angry."

FOR FURTHER REFLECTION

The Best Conflict Resolution Technique: How to have effective conflict resolution in your marriage. Monika Hoyt YouTube

Healing from Trauma!

CONNECTING WITH THE BOOK
* How can this story be helpful to you?
* How do you deal with painful memories?

CONNECTING WITH DAILY LIFE
* Have you or anyone you know ever experienced trauma (including molestation or rape)?
* How has this trauma affected you?
* How do you deal with these painful memories?
* Have you ever told anyone a painful truth and not been believed?
* What will or has helped you in your healing?
* (If you know a child who is being abused, contact Child Protective Services.)
* What do you think is important for a person to change from a victim state to a survivor?
* What do you think about the dream changing method?

WORDS TO LIVE BY
* "Trauma is personal. It does not disappear if it is not validated. When it is ignored or invalidated, the silent screams continue internally heard only by the one held captive. When someone enters the pain and hears the screams, healing can begin." Danielle Bernock

FOR FURTHER REFLECTION
Rape Crisis Centers and Hotlines and Child Protective Services

Anger Management!

CONNECTING WITH THE BOOK

❖ How can this story be helpful to you?

❖ What tools will help you with your anger?

CONNECTING WITH DAILY LIFE

❖ How would you describe your anger?

❖ When and how often do you get angry?

❖ On a scale of 0 to 10, how angry do you get?

❖ How long can you stay angry?

❖ Has your anger caused you or other people problems?

❖ Do you have road rage or rageful anger?

❖ What do you do when you get angry or emotionally upset?

❖ What causes you to become angry?

❖ What angry thoughts run through your mind?

❖ What do you think about Don's helpful tools? 1) Breathing calming breaths, 2) rotating the baseball in his hand, 3) saying his motto: "I'm thankful to be alive and I'm going to enjoy my drive," 4) smiling and looking at the little racoon, and 5) practicing, practicing, practicing?

❖ What will you do to effectively deal with your anger?

WORDS TO LIVE BY

❖ Respond to this statement by Alexander Pope:

"To be angry is to revenge the faults of others on ourselves."

FOR FURTHER REFLECTION

Anger management: 10 tips to tame your temper, The Mayo Clinic

He Told Me to Kill Myself!

CONNECTING WITH THE BOOK

- ❖ How can this story be helpful to you?
- ❖ What do you think is helpful in overcoming abuse?

CONNECTING WITH DAILY LIFE

- ❖ Have you or someone close to you been abused as a child?
- ❖ Did you or someone close to you who was abused get help?
- ❖ If not, why not?
- ❖ If so, what was helpful?
- ❖ What are lasting effects of child abuse?
- ❖ How do you see physical, sexual, and emotional abuse as being similar and different?
- ❖ What do you think about how Kim dealt with her abuser, her mother, and her date?
- ❖ What do you think about being glad the abuser was dead?
- ❖ What were the steps that you think were helpful to Kim?
- ❖ How do you think they were helpful?
- ❖ What do you think about speaking out to help others?

WORDS TO LIVE BY

- ❖ Respond to this statement by Maya Angelou:
  "You may not control all the events that happen to you, but you can decide not to be reduced by them."

FOR FURTHER REFLECTION

Children's Advocacy Centers
Child Protective Services (CPS)
Prevent Child Abuse America resources
Licensed Children's Therapists

I've Got to Get Marriage Right This Time!

CONNECTING WITH THE BOOK

❖ How can this story be helpful to you?

❖ What do you think causes and helps workaholics?

CONNECTING WITH DAILY LIFE

❖ How can the death of a child's parent affect one's life and relationships?

❖ How do messages from the surviving parent affect the child?

❖ How can stored grief have long-term effects?

❖ How does it help to have loving memories of the dead parent?

❖ How is it important to address the relationship with the parent and the loss?

❖ What are important boundaries to have with pushy parents?

❖ What do you think about the washcloth and towels as visual and physical tools?

❖ What do you think about how workaholism affects relationships?

❖ What do you think about the several changes involved in developing a good relationship?

❖ How can touching exercises help a couple's intimacy?

WORDS TO LIVE BY

❖ Respond to this statement by Cecelia Amen:

"We're not in this life just to work, we're in it to live."

FOR FURTHER REFLECTION

The Intimacy Jungle by Terry Parsons

Putting the Family Back Together!

CONNECTING WITH THE BOOK

❖ How can this story be helpful to you?

❖ What do you think families can do to improve their lives and relationships?

CONNECTING WITH DAILY LIFE

❖ How can you tell if the child (or any person) who appears strong on the outside, may be carrying a lot of pain?

❖ What do you think about the "super camera" or some other creative way to help the person access the pain inside the mind?

❖ What do you think about the use of clay as a way for a child (or an adult) to physically and emotionally express the story inside?

❖ What do you think about the family "falling apart" in the process?

❖ What do you think about the mom seeing and being moved by the scene?

❖ What do you think about the mom, brother, and Cody recreating their family with clay?

WORDS TO LIVE BY

❖ Respond to this statement by Laura Parsons, Registered Play Therapist:

"Children have not fully developed cognitively or emotionally, so they are not always able to express themselves verbally. Play helps them address issues at their developmental level."

FOR FURTHER REFLECTION

The Association for Play Therapy

Death of a Child!

CONNECTING WITH THE BOOK
- How can this story be helpful to you?
- What do you think about the greatest loss?

CONNECTING WITH DAILY LIFE
- Have you or someone close to you suffered the death of a child?
- If so, what is your story?
- What do you think is important or helpful for you or other parents whose child died from a particular cause?
- What do you think about "mourning partner?"
- What do you think about the stages of grief? 1) Shock or disbelief. 2) If only or Bargaining. 3) Depression. 4) Anger. 5) Acceptance. 6) Hope.
- What do you think about how Conner and Paige dealt with this process?
- What do you think about grief as being a lifetime process?
- What do you think about the fact that you really don't get over such a devastating grief, but you can get through it?
- What do you think about what parents can do to move on with their lives with meaning and healing?

WORDS TO LIVE BY
- Respond to this statement by Leo Tolstoy:
  "Only people who are capable of loving strongly can also suffer great sorrow, but this same necessity of loving serves to counteract their grief and heals them."

FOR FURTHER REFLECTION
Grief Support Groups—Some focus on a particular cause of death or age of the child.
Healing Hearts: Baby Loss Comfort

The Struggling Recovering Alcoholic!

CONNECTING WITH THE BOOK

❖ How can this story be helpful to you?

❖ What do you think about alcoholism?

CONNECTING WITH DAILY LIFE

❖ Do you or someone you know have an alcohol problem?

❖ What do you think causes alcoholism or addictions?

❖ If you have an alcohol problem or an addiction, how would you describe it and how do you deal with it?

❖ Have you attended any Twelve Step or other recover program?

❖ What do you think are keys for alcoholics and addicts recovering?

❖ How can sponsors and therapists help?

❖ How do you think prayer and "On my knees to retrieve my keys" can help?

❖ What do you think about the effect of "don't feel" on a person?

❖ What do you think about "one day at a time?"

❖ If someone close to you is an alcoholic or addict, what do you think you can do to be helpful?

WORDS TO LIVE BY

❖ The World Health Organization defines alcoholism (alcohol abuse disorder or AUD is the current diagnostic term) as "any drinking which results in problems."

FOR FURTHER REFLECTION

Good Resources: Alcoholics Anonymous, The National Institute on Alcohol Abuse and Alcoholism (NIAAA), The Mayo Clinic, Addiction Specialists.

Coming Out!

CONNECTING WITH THE BOOK

❖ How can this story be helpful to you?

❖ What are your thoughts about sexual orientation?

CONNECTING WITH DAILY LIFE

❖ What are your thoughts about homosexuality?

❖ How did you form these views?

❖ What do you think about the messages Warren was given about homosexuality and how they affected him?

❖ What do you think the Bible says about homosexuality?

❖ What do you think about Warren's response to what Jesus said or did not say about homosexuality?

❖ What do you know about how the term has been translated through the centuries and in modern times?

❖ What are your thoughts about various societal views of homosexuality?

❖ What are your thoughts about scientific studies regarding causes of sexual orientation?

❖ If you struggle with sexual orientation issues, I strongly encourage you to get the help you need.

❖ What do you think about each of the issues and the combination of issues Warren presented?

❖ What do think about Warren and other "Warrens?"

WORDS TO LIVE BY

❖ Respond to this statement from Paul in Romans 8:38-39:
"For I am convinced that...not anything in all creation will be able to separate us from the love of God..."

FOR FURTHER REFLECTION

What Scientists Know—and Don't Know—About Sexual Orientation, in <u>Psychological Science in the Public Interest</u> published by the Association for Psychological Science

The Bi-Polar Clown!

CONNECTING WITH THE BOOK

❖ How can this story be helpful to you?

❖ What do you think will help people better understand mental illness?

CONNECTING WITH DAILY LIFE

❖ Do you or someone you know suffer from depression or bi-polar disorder?

❖ What is important to understand about the various types and levels of depression?

❖ What can be helpful for depression and bi-polar disorder?

❖ Do you know helpful resources for people with mental illness?

❖ What do you think about the pastor, his wife, and what the church did?

❖ What do you think about Jill's faith and even praying for the minister after he harshly judged her?

❖ What do you think about the power of courage?

❖ What do you think about Jill and Happy Clown?

❖ How do you respond when a person close to you dies?

WORDS TO LIVE BY

❖ Jill said: "Maybe I'll go back to that church. It is God's house; not the preacher's church. God knows my depression is not of the devil. I believe God will give me strength."

FOR FURTHER REFLECTION

NAMI, the National Alliance on Mental Illness is the nation's largest grassroots mental health organization dedicated to building better lives for the millions of Americans affected by mental illness.

Made in the USA
Coppell, TX
19 December 2019

13343369R10089